CALIFORNIA DREAM CYCLING

text, maps
and lettering
by CHUCK
"BODFISH"
ELLIOT
illustrations
by LISA JO
SEDLACEK

D1738352

CONTINUING THE
GOOD ROADS CAMPAIGN

THE BATTLE FOR GOOD ROADS WAS INITIATED BY CALIFORNIA CYCLISTS ONE HUNDRED YEARS AGO. THIS "GOOD ROADS CAMPAIGN" BROUGHT THE NEED FOR OIL-SURFACED AND PAVED ROADWAYS INTO THE PUBLIC SPOTLIGHT, EFFECTIVELY KICKING INTO GEAR A MOVEMENT WHICH EVENTUALLY RESULTED IN THE WORLD'S FINEST SYSTEM OF PUBLIC ROADWAYS.

"THERE IS NO DOUBT THAT THE GENERAL INTERESTS OF THE STATE WOULD GAIN BY THE SUCCESS OF THE PLAN WHICH THE WHEELMEN PROPOSE FOR THE IMPROVE-MENT OF THE COUNTRY ROADS ... IT IS OBVIOUS THAT GOOD ROADS WOULD HELP PRODUCTION AND TRADE AS WELL AS FACILITATE THE PLEASURE OF BICYCLING."
- S.F. CHRONICLE 2/24/1896

"THE INFLUENCE OF THE BICYCLE UPON THIS AGITATION FOR IMPROVED HIGHWAYS CANNOT BE OVERESTIMATED, IT IS DUE MORE DIRECTLY TO THE EFFORTS OF THE WHEELMEN THAN TO ANY OTHER ONE CAUSE. ANY MACHINE WHICH ENABLES A MAN TO TRAVEL WITH PLEASURE, WITHOUT DISCOMFORT AND PRACTICALLY WITHOUT EXPENSE, FORTY MILES A DAY, IS EVIDENTLY ONE WHICH HAS COME TO STAY."
-BUREAU OF CALIFORNIA HWYS BULLETIN, DIRECTOR R.C. IRVINE — 1896

A FEW CALIFORNIA COUNTIES HAVE RECENTLY MADE MOVEMENTS TOWARD THE BANNING OF BICYCLES AND GROUPS OF CYCLISTS ON PUBLIC ROADWAYS — BE EVER VIGILANT, GET INVOLVED IN COUNTY POLITICS, PRESERVE THE ROADS FOR CYCLISTS!

with help from:

MY FELLOW DREAM CYCLERS: LISA SEDLACEK, COLBY JOE, DON RICE, STEVE AND KATY O'BRYAN, ED HURLEY, JACK WALDORF, NORTON BELL, GREG AND WENDY AT OVERLAND EQUIPMENT, JOHN NEWMAN, KEITH BENNETT, DR. GEORGE BARAKAT, BERNIE AND JO ANN McCOY, PETER MASSOLETTI, LAURI RUPPERT, JIM AND CATHY HAAGEN-SMIT, ED CALDWELL AND DON SERAO.
SPECIAL THANKS TO ROGER WALDEN FOR THE COVER PHOTO.

PUBLISHED BY BODFISH BOOKS
          P.O. BOX 69
          CHESTER, CALIFORNIA 96020

PRINTED ON RECYCLED PAPER BY:
          ED'S PRINTING
          550 CHERRY ST.
          CHICO, CA. 95926

books by BODFISH

I.S.B.N. 0-9616709-0-9

10 9 8 7 6 5 4 3 2 1st PRINTING

CONTENTS

CONTENTS CONT.

CALIFORNIA DREAM CYCLING

WE ALL HAVE DIFFERENT IDEAS ABOUT WHAT THE IDEAL BIKE RIDE IS MADE OF. YOUR LIST OF INGREDIENTS MAY INCLUDE SMOOTH ROAD SURFACES, PAVED SHOULDERS, RUNNING STREAMS AND LUSH VEGETATION ALONG MUCH OF THE ROUTE. OTHER COMPONENTS MAY INCLUDE SWEEPING VISTAS, FREQUENT SWIMMING HOLES, INFREQUENT MOTOR TRAFFIC, STRONG OR TALKATIVE RIDING COMPANIONS OR COUNTRYSIDE WHERE THE ONLY NOISE IS THE WHIRRING OF SPOKES ACCOMPANIED BY "BIRD JAZZ".

INCREDIBLY, MANY CALIFORNIA CYCLISTS ARE WILLING TO PUT UP WITH TIGHTROPING THE OUTER EDGE OF A VIBRATING RIBBON OF HEAVILY TRAVELLED ASPHALT. OTHERS HAVE SWORN OFF ROAD RIDING AND WILL RIDE NOTHING BUT DIRT.

MY RECIPE MAY SEEM A BIT EXTREME TO THE URBAN CYCLIST BUT, AFTER TWENTY YEARS OF CYCLING CALIFORNIA ROADWAYS, I BELIEVE THE MOST IMPORTANT INGREDIENT IN A GREAT BIKE RIDE IS THE QUIET ROAD. SURFACE QUALITY CONCERNS ME LESS — I HAVE TIRES, WHEELS AND BIKES THAT WILL EASILY HANDLE ALL TYPES OF ROAD SURFACES.

I HAVE THESE RECURRENT DREAMS THAT SHOW ME RIDING THROUGH PARK-LIKE FORESTS ACCOMPANIED BY CRYSTAL CLEAR STREAMS LINED WITH SUCCULENT PLANT LIFE, ASPEN GROVES, VELVET MEADOWS AND NARROW MACADAM LANES THAT ROLL ON AND ON WITHOUT END... BIRDS ARE CALLING, FROGS BELCHING AND A COOL WIND FEATHERS MY CHEEK. WOVEN THROUGH THIS SCENE IS THE PIANO MUSIC — A "LIFE IS BLISS" LULLABY THAT CAUSES THE ASPEN LEAVES AND PINE NEEDLES TO TWITTER... AS IF THEY'RE EXPERIENCING AN UNCONTROLLABLE ORGASM.

I WENT OUT LOOKING FOR THE 'DREAM RIDES', FROM THE UNDERBELLY TO THE SUPERIOR END OF THE STATE OF CALIFORNIA — MOSTLY LOOPS, OFTEN HILLY RIDES THAT MAKE YOU SWEAT — RIDES THAT LET YOU SING!

RIDING IS THERAPUTIC FOR MANY OF US. GOOD RIDES SOFTEN OUR ANGER TOWARD THE RAT RACE; THEY HELP BUILD ANTIBODIES THAT PROTECT US FROM THE RUDE AND INCONSIDERATE OAFS AROUND US. A GREAT TWO OR THREE HOUR SPIN RESETS OUR HORIZONTAL HOLD, STOPS THE HOURS FROM FLUTTERING HYPNOTICALLY PAST OUR EYES... TEACHING US BALANCE AND THE VALUE OF FORWARD MOTION, AS WE STRIVE TO IMPROVE, REFINE AND SMOOTH OUT OUR CYCLICAL IMPERFECTIONS.

CYCLING TRAINS US TO BE HUMBLE. WE ARE SLIGHT, SOFT AND VULNERABLE AT THE ROAD'S EDGE. NEARLY EVERY CALIFORNIA COUNTY HAS THE "PHENOM" SKINNY KID ON TWO WHEELS WHO'LL CATCH YOU ON A HILL AND INJECT CONCRETE IN YOUR THIGHS AS HE REELS HIMSELF DEFTLY TO THE CREST.

CYCLING MAY BE GOOD FOR THE LUNGS, CIRCULATORY SYSTEM AND THE BRAIN (AS CLAIMED IN CYCLING PERIODICALS), BUT IT IS MOST ASSUREDLY GOOD FOR THE SOUL. A GOOD RIDE ALLOWS YOU TO TALK WITH YOURSELF, SING TO THE PRAIRIE DOGS OR GOLDEN MANTLED GROUND SQUIRRELS AND MOST IMPORTANTLY — TO BECOME MINDLESS. FOOT TWIDDLING UNTANGLES THE DAY'S FRUSTRATIONS, CLEANS THE DIGESTIVE SYSTEM OF UNWANTED ACIDS AND SLUGGISH FREIGHT.

MY GRANDFATHER SAT IN HIS PORCH ROCKER TWIDDLING HIS THUMBS LOOKING OUT OVER THE GARDEN FOR AN HOUR OR SO EVERY EVENING. THIS BEHAVOIR UNNERVED GRANDMOTHER, BUT SHE KNEW BETTER THAN TO INTERRUPT. GRANDFATHER WAS AN EVEN-TEMPERED "SATISFIED MAN" WHO ALWAYS TOOK TIME TO TEASE AND GAME WITH HIS GRANDCHILDREN. THIS SMILING MAN KNEW THE VALUE OF AN EVENING RIDE.

WHAT'S A BODFISH?

I'M A MAP GUY; I CAN SIT FOR HOURS ABSORBING TOPOGRAPHICAL LINES, ROADS, CREEK DRAINAGES AND TRAILS FROM A WELL-MADE MAP. I ALSO LOVE DRAWING MAPS. FOR THE BEST RESULTS I KEEP THE MAPS STRAIGHTFORWARD AND SIMPLE. I ALSO RECOMMEND THAT YOU CARRY THE APPROPRIATE COUNTY OR AUTO CLUB MAPS TO USE ALONG WITH MY SKETCH.

IN THE TEXT I REFUSE TO "TALK YOU THROUGH" THE ENTIRE LOOP — TELLING YOU WHEN TO TURN LEFT, RIGHT OR WARNING YOU OF EACH HILLCLIMB. SOME OF YOU MAY THINK THIS INFO MAKES FOR PRETTY EXCITING READING... I THINK NOT.

THIS BOOK LEANS TOWARD THE PAVED ROUTES, SOME OF WHICH MAY BE MORE PLEASURABLE IF EXECUTED ON A FAT BIKE. THE ROAD SURFACES VARY, THE SCENERY MAY NOT ALWAYS BE YOUR FAVORITE, BUT WE HAVE KEPT YOU ABOVE THE DESERTS AND OUT OF THE HEAVILY-TRAMPLED FLATLANDS WHERE YOU ARE MOST LIKELY TO ENCOUNTER THE MOTORING HOARD, THICK BROWN AIR AND MONOTONOUS SCENERY.

BODFISH IS ACTUALLY A TEAM, NOT A PERSON. WHENEVER YOU SEE THE NAME BODFISH THINK "TEAM BODFISH." MY BEST BUDDY LISA SEDLACEK AND I HAVE BEEN EXPLORING THE BACKROADS OF CALIFORNIA (AND THE BACK-ROADS OF NORTH AMERICA, FOR THAT MATTER) FOR FIFTEEN YEARS. WE'VE WRITTEN, MAPPED, ILLUSTRATED AND PUB-LISHED FOUR BICYCLE GUIDES: <u>BUTTE COUNTRY BICYCLE JOURNEYS</u>, <u>CYCLING IN THE SHADOW OF SHASTA</u>, <u>CYCLING THE CALIFORNIA OUTBACK</u> AND THIS VOLUME — <u>CALIFORNIA DREAM CYCLING</u>.

TEAM BODFISH RECENTLY ADDED A THIRD MEMBER, "THE LITTLE FISH" COLBY JOSEPH ELLIOT. COLBY HAS PUT IN QUITE A FEW "CABOOSE" MILES DURING HIS FIRST SIX MONTHS. HE'S ONE MORE REASON FOR US TO STAY HEALTHY AND ON THE BIKES.

HOW THIS BOOK WORKS

THIS GUIDE IS DIVIDED INTO THREE SECTIONS —
COAST RANGE LOOPS, FOOTHILL RIDES AND HIGH COUNTRY
TRIPS. WE START IN THE SOUTH (SAN DIEGO COUNTY) AND
WORK NORTH (TO SISKIYOU COUNTY). YOU'RE UNDOUBTEDLY
GOING TO FEEL WE MISSED A FEW GREAT RIDES IN THIS 1000
MILE STRETCH — POSSIBLY YOUR FAVORITE LOOP. WE CHOSE NOT
TO DEAL WITH FLATLAND LOOPS IN THIS VOLUME AND WE
DROPPED MANY PROSPECTIVE LOOPS DUE TO HEAVY TRAFFIC.

IT'S NOT EASY TO FIND ENTIRE LOOPS IN
SOUTHERN CALIFORNIA SUITABLE FOR A BOOK ON DREAM
CYCLING. YET, WE FOUND A LOOP EAST OF SAN DIEGO THAT
SURPRIZED US — TALL TREES, RUNNING WATER AND GREAT
VIEWS. WE WERE CAREFUL NOT TO RIDE THESE ROADS DURING
HOLIDAYS, WEEKENDS OR DURING HUNTING SEASON.

AT THE END OF THIS BOOK WE MAKE QUICK
MENTION ABOUT THE RIDES THAT ALMOST MADE IT INTO OUR TOP
FORTY. MANY OF THESE WERE ON THE FRINGES OF URBAN
AREAS AND WE WERE CONCERNED THAT THEY WOULD NOT REMAIN
EXCELLENT RIDES THROUGHOUT THE NINETEEN-NINETIES.

BETWEEN SAN DIEGO AND LOS ANGELES WE "DIS-
COVERED" A LOOP WEST OF TEMECULA AND NORTH OF FALLBROOK
THAT PROBES A GROVE OF AVOCADOS AND PRESENTS A FEW
CHALLENGING CLIMBS (WATCH THOSE SLICK CREEK CROSSINGS
AT THE BOTTOM). WE ARE BETTING THAT THIS WILL REMAIN AS
ONE OF "SO CAL'S" MOST PLEASANT ROAD RIDES INTO THE 21ST
CENTURY. "ACCEPTABLE ROADS," ESPECIALLY ENTIRE LOOPS,
WERE NOT TO BE FOUND IN THE L.A. BASIN OR THE "INLAND
EMPIRE" (RIVERSIDE). THIS JUDGEMENT IS RELATIVE TO YOUR
EXPERIENCE — REMEMBER, I'M A COUNTRY BOY FROM THE
NORTH.

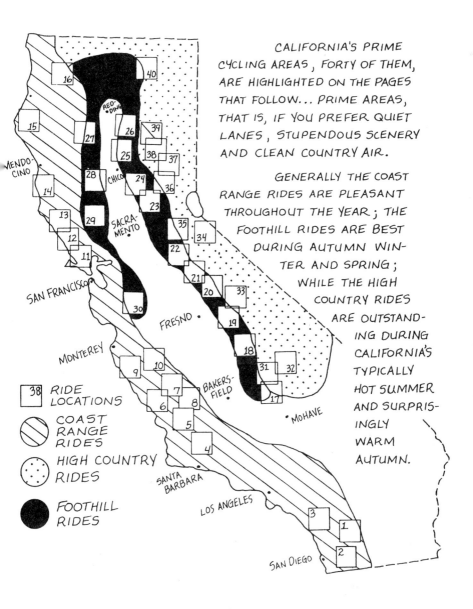

CALIFORNIA'S PRIME CYCLING AREAS, FORTY OF THEM, ARE HIGHLIGHTED ON THE PAGES THAT FOLLOW... PRIME AREAS, THAT IS, IF YOU PREFER QUIET LANES, STUPENDOUS SCENERY AND CLEAN COUNTRY AIR.

GENERALLY THE COAST RANGE RIDES ARE PLEASANT THROUGHOUT THE YEAR; THE FOOTHILL RIDES ARE BEST DURING AUTUMN WINTER AND SPRING; WHILE THE HIGH COUNTRY RIDES ARE OUTSTANDING DURING CALIFORNIA'S TYPICALLY HOT SUMMER AND SURPRISINGLY WARM AUTUMN.

38 RIDE LOCATIONS

COAST RANGE RIDES

HIGH COUNTRY RIDES

FOOTHILL RIDES

TIMING IS EVERYTHING

CYCLING IS A YEAR-ROUND SPORT IN CALIFORNIA. WINTER CAN BE A GREAT TIME FOR EXPLORING ANY OF THE TWENTY COASTAL LOOPS WE'VE MAPPED HERE. SPRING IS OUTSTANDING IN THE FOOTHILLS — VERDANT FOLDS OF THE NORTH AMERICAN PLATE COLLIDING WITH THE PACIFIC PLATE, PEPPERED WITH (SOMETIMES SMOTHERED BY) WILDFLOWERS.

SUMMER OFTEN FINDS THE LOWER PORTIONS OF THE COASTAL ROUTES SOCKED-IN WITH FOG — A GOOD TIME TO BE EXPLORING THE CALIFORNIA HIGH COUNTRY. AUTUMN IS AN EXCELLENT TIME TO BE CYCLING ANY OF THE THREE ZONES PRESENTED HERE.

AMONG THE REASONS FOR BUYING A CYCLING GUIDEBOOK ARE THE HOPES OF AVOIDING TRAFFIC, FINDING OUT ABOUT: CAMPGROUNDS, TOWNS WITH SERVICES, WATER AVAILABILITY AND TO FIND THE IDEAL RIDE WITHOUT HAVING TO EXPERIMENT OR EXPLORE ON YOUR OWN.

WE'VE SCOUTED THE QUIET AND SCENIC LOOPS FOR YOU AND SUGGESTED PEAK SEASONS FOR EXECUTING THESE JOURNEYS. ONE THING YOU MUST REALIZE, HOWEVER, IS THAT ALL RIDES WILL INVOLVE MORE TRAFFIC DURING WEEKENDS — ESPECIALLY HOLIDAY WEEKENDS — THAN ON WEEKDAYS. IF YOU HAVE WEEKENDS ONLY FOR CYCLING BE SURE TO BEGIN YOUR RIDE EARLY IN THE DAY (ESPECIALLY GOOD ADVICE DURING THE SUMMER MONTHS) YOU WILL AVOID BOTH HEAT AND TRAFFIC.

FAT TIRES OR SKINNY?

      SLIDING ALONG THE TARMAC ON 120 POUND PER SQUARE INCH TIRES IS THE SECOND BEST SENSATION I'VE FOUND IN THE WORLD OF OUTDOOR SPORTS. I GET NEARLY THE SAME THRILL OUT OF RIDING 60 P.S.I. FAT TIRES ON THE SAME CIRCUIT.

      I INVESTED MUCH OF THE '70's ROAD BIKING... SEARCHING OUT THE FINEST ROADS IN THE WEST... PAVED ROADS. SOME WERE GREAT; MANY WERE NOT SO GOOD — 98% OF THE TIME THE BIG NEGATIVE ON A ROAD RIDE WAS TRAFFIC. SO, NATURALLY, WE USED FATTER TIRES AND RODE LESS AND LESS ON PAVEMENT WHICH LED TO THE PUBLISHING OF <u>CYCLING THE CALIFORNIA OUTBACK</u>.

      AFTER A DEEP SWING THROUGH THE WORLD OF OFFROAD RIDING MY LOVE FOR ROAD RIDING HAS ONCE AGAIN BEEN FANNED INTO A FIRESTORM OF ENTHUSIASM. IT'S ALL CYCLING ; IT'S ALL LUNGS, HEART, THIGHS AND ENDORPHINS — JUST KEEP ME ON THE BACKROADS. SURE, YOU CAN DE-SENSITIZE THE NERVOUS SYSTEM TO THE POINT WHERE YOU HARDLY FLINCH AT 60 MPH CLOSE-CALLS WITH THE MOTORING PUBLIC, BUT WHO NEEDS THAT!

COAST RANGE RIDES

STARTING IN THE SOUTH AND RIDING NORTH TEAM BODFISH HAS SNIFFED OUT THE QUIET AND SCENIC ROAD JOURNEYS BETWEEN THE MEXICAN AND OREGON BORDERS, FROM SAN DIEGO TO SISKIYOU COUNTY. THE 21 LOOPS SKETCHED HERE RANGE BETWEEN 8 AND 100 MILES, AVERAGING 40 MILES PER RIDE.

DURING THE WRITING AND DESIGNING OF THIS VOLUME WE DECIDED TO ELIMINATE A FEW LOOPS IN VENTURA, ORANGE AND L.A. COUNTIES. THEY JUST DIDN'T MEASURE UP. ONLY QUIET, CLEAN AIR, COUNTRY RIDES SURVIVED THE FINAL CUT.

WHILE VISITING RELATIVES IN THE LOS ANGELES AREA WE'VE FOUND A FEW HALF-WAY DECENT RIDES INTO THE RESIDENTIAL HILLS THAT RISE OUT OF CONGESTED URBAN VALLEYS. ONE LOOP WE'VE FOUND TO BE TOLERABLE EARLY ON SUNDAYS IS A CIRCUIT AROUND THE VERDUGO MTNS. THE HIGHLIGHT FOR US ON THIS LOOP IS THE WEAVING, CLIMBING ROUTE THROUGH THE GLENDALE HIGHLANDS ALONG ROADS NAMED VALENTINE, WONDERVIEW, RIMCREST, STARVALE, MELWOOD, OLD PHILLIPS AND SUNSHINE DRIVE. WE LOVE HILLS, PULLING UP IN THE CLIPS, POSTING, HONKING AND FEELING THE BLOOD RUSHING INTO THE THIGHS.

THE COAST RANGE RIDES ARE ON ROADS THAT ARE GENERALLY OPEN YEAR AROUND, UNLESS THE RARE COLD STORM HAS DROPPED DOWN FROM THE GULF OF ALASKA AND DUMPED SNOW ON THE HIGH RIDGES OF HUMBOLDT, MENDOCINO, SONOMA AND EVEN SAN DIEGO COUNTIES.

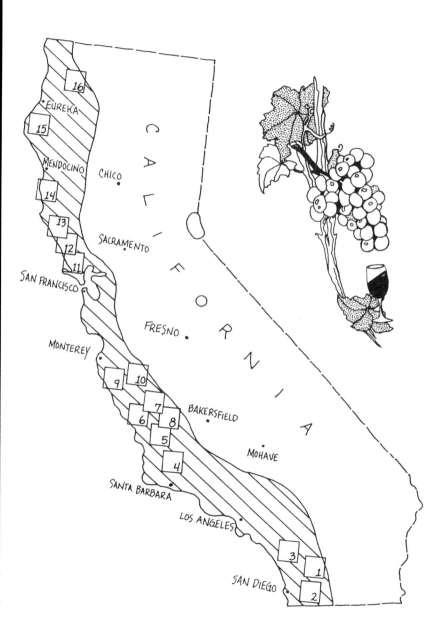

16

EUREKA

15

MENDOCINO   CHICO

14

13

12

11

SAN FRANCISCO

C A L I F O R N I A

SACRAMENTO

FRESNO

MONTEREY

9   10

7

6   8

BAKERSFIELD

5

4

MOHAVE

SANTA BARBARA

LOS ANGELES

3

1

SAN DIEGO

2

1

SAN DIEGO COUNTY

MT. LAGUNA

RIDING THIS LOOP IN A COUNTERCLOCKWISE DIRECTION FROM THE SUMMIT OF HWY 79, NEAR THE PARK HEADQUARTERS OR PASO PICACHO CAMPGROUNDS (HOT SHOWERS), SEEMS TO BE THE BEST APPROACH.

THE ONLY STRETCH OF ROADWAY WHERE TRAFFIC COULD BE A PROBLEM WOULD BE THE CANYON SECTION OF HWY 79 SOUTH OF THE PARK HEADQUARTERS. ENJOY THIS 1500' DROP DURING EARLY MORNING HOURS AND YOU'LL SEE VERY FEW MOTORISTS.

> STARTING POINT —
> CUYAMACA RANCHO STATE PARK — PASO PICACHO CAMP.
>
> DISTANCE —
> 50 MILES
>
> DIRECTION —
> COUNTERCLOCKWISE
>
> HIGH POINT —
> 6,001' AT LAGUNA MTN.
>
> LOW POINT —
> 3,539' AT SAMAGATUMA

SHORTLY AFTER CROSSING SAMAGATUMA CREEK YOU'LL TURN LEFT (THE NEWLY-PAVED HWY 79 TURNS RIGHT) ON AN OLD POORLY-MAINTAINED PAVED ROAD TO GUATAY AND PINE VALLEY OVER THE NORTH SHOULDER OF GUATAY MOUNTAIN.

A MILE OR SO SOUTHEAST OF A BUSTLING PINE VALLEY ROAD S-1 (THE SUNRISE HWY) BEGINS A TWELVE MILE CLIMB TOWARD THE LAGUNA MTN. TRADING POST. BE SURE YOUR WATER BOTTLES ARE FULL BEFORE COMMENCING THE CLIMB, THIS IS A HOT DRY CANYON (SCOVE CANYON).

THE ROAD LEVELS OUT MOMENTARILY IN CROUCH VALLEY (THE MEADOWS INFORMATION STATION IS HERE) BEFORE SENDING YOU UP INTO THE TREES.... AH, THE COOL SCENT OF MOUNTAIN PINE. YOU'LL SHORTLY COME UPON THE LAGUNA MTN. TRADING POST — A GREAT PLACE FOR LUNCH. JUST BEYOND THE TRADING POST YOU'LL CLIMB SLIGHTLY TO THE HIGH POINT OF THE RIDE (JUST OVER 6,000'). BE SURE TO SWING INTO ONE OF THE OVERLOOK AREAS FOR A VIEW OF THE DESERT.

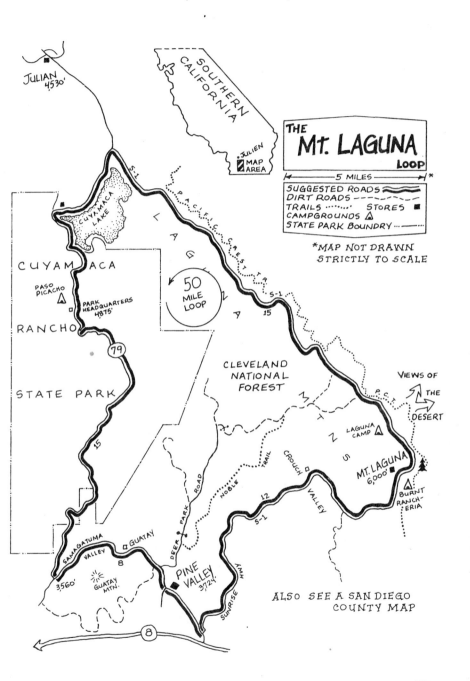

SOUTHERN CALIFORNIA

JULIAN
4,530'

JULIEN
MAP AREA

THE Mt. LAGUNA LOOP

— 5 MILES —

SUGGESTED ROADS
DIRT ROADS
TRAILS
CAMPGROUNDS △
STATE PARK BOUNDRY
STORES ■

*MAP NOT DRAWN STRICTLY TO SCALE

CUYAMACA LAKE

S-1

P
A
C
I
F
I
C

C
R
E
S
T

T
R

L
A
G
U
N
A
S

CUYAMACA

PASO PICACHO △

PARK HEADQUARTERS 4875'

RANCHO

79

50 MILE LOOP

S-1

15

STATE PARK

15

CLEVELAND NATIONAL FOREST

VIEWS OF

THE DESERT

P.C.T.

LAGUNA CAMP △

MT. LAGUNA 6,000' ■

BURNT RANCH-ERIA △

M
T
N
S

N
O
B
L
E

T
R
A
I
L

CROUCH VALLEY

12

S-1

DEER PARK ROAD

SAMAGATUMA VALLEY

GUATAY

8

3,560'

GUATAY MTN.

PINE VALLEY 3,724' ■

SUNRISE HWY

ALSO SEE A SAN DIEGO COUNTY MAP

8

2

SAN DIEGO COUNTY

ALPINE SOUTH

THE CANYONS ABOVE THE SINGING HILLS COUNTRY CLUB ARE FALLING PREY TO THE DEVELOPER'S BULLDOZERS... AND IN A BIG HURRY. A FRIEND TOLD ME OF THIS LOOP TEN YEARS AGO, "A QUIET LOOP WITH TREES, A BIT OF SHADE IN THE CANYONS AND AN OCCASIONAL RANCH."

THERE ARE MORE TREES THAN YOU MIGHT EXPECT THIS CLOSE TO THE MEXICAN BORDER, BUT THE "OCCASIONAL" RANCH HAS BECOME THE MORE FREQUENT RANCHETTE. ON THE LOWER (WEST END) OF THIS LOOP DEVELOPMENT, FEVER HAS A FIRM GRIP ON THE LOCALS.

YOU MIGHT START THIS LOOP BY PARKING NEAR THE CORNER OF WILLOW GLEN DRIVE AND DEHASA ROAD, RIDING DOWN WILLOW GLEN IN THE EARLY MORNING (ONLY GOLFERS DRIVE THIS STRETCH DURING THESE HOURS), THEN CLIMBING INTO THE HILLS OF THIS CIRCUIT IN A COUNTERCLOCKWISE DIRECTION... STEELE CANYON AND JAMUL DRIVE.

A GREAT WINTERTIME RIDE — ON A WEEKDAY, IF YOU CAN SWING IT.

STARTING POINTS —
SINGING HILLS COUNTRY CLUB
OR ALPINE

DISTANCE —
42 MILES

DIRECTION —
COUNTERCLOCKWISE

HIGH POINT — 2501' NEAR
THE JAPATUL FIRE STATION

LOW POINT — 350' AT
STEELE CANYON ROAD

LODGING — BEST FOUND IN
ALPINE

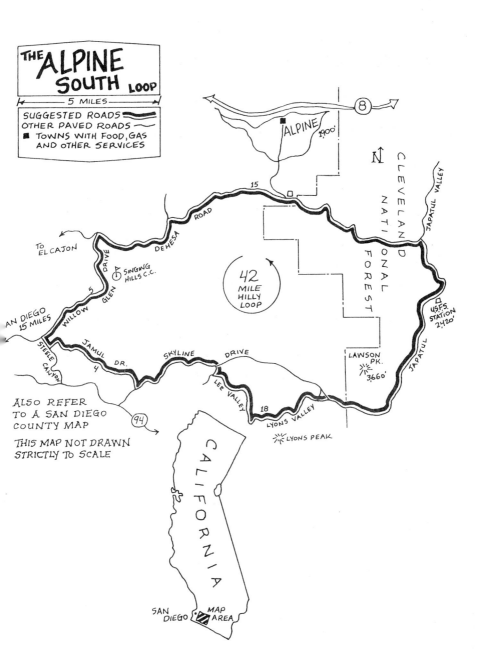

THE **ALPINE** SOUTH **LOOP**

|←——— 5 MILES ———→|

SUGGESTED ROADS
OTHER PAVED ROADS
■ TOWNS WITH FOOD, GAS
  AND OTHER SERVICES

8

ALPINE 1,900'

Ñ

CLEVELAND NATIONAL FOREST

JAPATUL VALLEY

15

DEMESA ROAD

TO EL CAJON

DRIVE

WILLOW GLEN

5

SINGING HILLS C.C.

42 MILE HILLY LOOP

U.S.F.S. STATION 2,420'

AN DIEGO 15 MILES

STEELE CANYON

JAMUL DR.

4

SKYLINE

DRIVE

LAWSON PK. 3,660'

JAPATUL

LEE VALLEY

18

LYONS VALLEY

LYONS PEAK

ALSO REFER TO A SAN DIEGO COUNTY MAP

THIS MAP NOT DRAWN STRICTLY TO SCALE

94

C A L I F O R N I A

SAN DIEGO

MAP AREA

19

3

SAN DIEGO AND RIVERSIDE COUNTIES
SANDIA CANYON

START THIS RIDE IN DOWNTOWN FALLBROOK. PARK ON ALVARADO BETWEEN MISSION AND MAIN (THERE'S A BIKE SHOP ON THIS BLOCK). RIDE NORTH ON PICO (STARTS OFF WITH A STEEP LITTLE UPHILL) WHICH BECOMES DE LUZ ROAD WITHIN A FEW BLOCKS. AT THE NORTH EDGE OF TOWN DE LUZ DROPS ABRUPTLY INTO THE CANYON OF THE SYCAMORE-LINED SANTA MARGARITA RIVER (ANY CREEK THAT FLOWS YEAR 'ROUND IN SO. CAL. DESERVES THE TITLE OF "RIVER").

STARTING POINT —
  FALLBROOK
DISTANCE —
  30 MILES
DIRECTION —
  COUNTERCLOCKWISE
HIGH POINT —
  1,501' ON THE RIDGE AT
  THE NORTH END OF LOOP
LOW POINT —
  240' ON THE SANTA
  MARGARITA RIVER
LODGING —
  FALLBROOK OR TEMECULA
BIKE SHOP —
  DOWNTOWN FALLBROOK

IF YOU TAKE MY ADVICE AND RIDE THIS IN A COUNTER-CLOCKWISE DIRECTION YOU'LL BE TURNING RIGHT ON A LONELY-LOOKING, LITTLE OFFSHOOT NAMED SANDIA CREEK ROAD — THIS GEM SERVES UP SOME RUDE LITTLE HILLS IN THE BEGINNING THAT ARE THANKFULLY SHORT — THE SURFACE ON THE BACKSIDES OF THESE IS PATCHY SO WATCH YOURSELF.

NOW YOU ARE IN AVOCADO LAND. THE GROVES ARE SLOWLY BEING REPLACED BY EXPENSIVE RANCHETTES, AND THE PAVEMENT IS NEW SO THE TRAFFIC IS ON THE INCREASE. ON THE NORTH END OF THIS LOOP YOU CLIMB TO THE HIGHEST POINT (A RIDGE OVERLOOKING TEMECULA AND A BOOMING RIVERSIDE CO.).

TURN LEFT AT THE TOP OF AVIENDA DEL ORO AND CLIMB TO THE JUNCTION OF MURRIETA ROAD BEFORE DROPPING BACK INTO SANDIA CANYON IN ROUTE TO DE LUZ. FOR THE NEXT HALF DOZEN MILES YOU'LL ENCOUNTER A HANDFUL OF CONCRETE PAD CREEK CROSSINGS THAT ARE TREACHEROUS — COVERED WITH ALGAE AND INCREDIBLY SLICK, HIT THEM STRAIGHT — DON'T BRAKE!

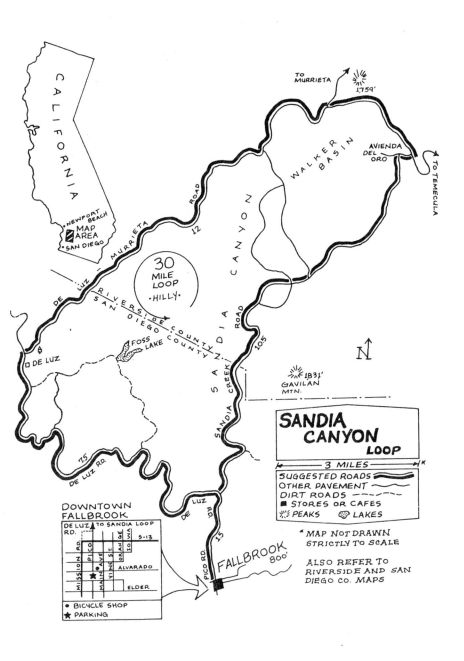

CALIFORNIA

Newport Beach
MAP AREA
San Diego

TO MURRIETA

1759'

WALKER BASIN

AVIENDA DEL ORO

TO TEMECULA

ROAD 12

SANDIA CANYON

DE LUZ - MURRIETA

RIVERSIDE COUNTY
SAN DIEGO COUNTY

30 MILE LOOP
·HILLY·

FOSS LAKE

ROAD 105

1831'
GAVILAN MTN.

N

DE LUZ

SANDIA CREEK ROAD

7.5
DE LUZ RD.

DE LUZ RD.

15

SANDIA CANYON LOOP

|← 3 MILES →|×

SUGGESTED ROADS
OTHER PAVEMENT
DIRT ROADS - - - -
■ STORES OR CAFES
☀ PEAKS ⊛ LAKES

* MAP NOT DRAWN STRICTLY TO SCALE

ALSO REFER TO RIVERSIDE AND SAN DIEGO CO. MAPS

DOWNTOWN FALLBROOK

DE LUZ RD.   TO SANDIA LOOP RD.
5-13
MISSION | PICO AVE | VINE ST. | ORANGE | 10 WY.
MAIN AVE
ALVARADO
ELDER

● BICYCLE SHOP
★ PARKING

FALLBROOK 800'

PICO RD.

DE LUZ RD.

21

4

CACHUMA SADDLE

THIS LOOP INVOLVES SOME GREAT CLIMBING (AND WE ALL LOVE CLIMBING). IF YOU RIDE IN A COUNTERCLOCKWISE DIRECTION, AS SUGGESTED, YOU'LL GET SOME WARM-UP MILES BEFORE ANY MAJOR CLIMBING. THIS WILL ALSO PRESENT THE ROUGH PAVEMENT TO YOU ON THE UPHILL AND SAVE THE SMOOTH STUFF FOR THE DESCENT.

THE CACHUMA SADDLE IS NOT AT THE TOP OF THE CLIMB. YOU'LL TAKE A LEFT AT THE RANGER STATION AND CLIMB MORE — TO THE SHOULDER OF RANGER PEAK — BEFORE BEGINNING THE WILD AND WOOLEY FIGUEROA MOUNTAIN DOWNHILL. A SIDE TRIP DEEPER INTO THE SAN RAFAEL MOUNTAINS, NORTH FROM THE CACHUMA SADDLE TO THE END OF THE PAVEMENT ON SUNSET VALLEY RD, WILL ADD TEN MILES AND A FEW HUNDRED EXTRA FEET OF CLIMBING TO YOUR JOURNEY.

SOLVANG (A SMALL VILLAGE JUST SOUTH OF THIS LOOP) HAS BEEN HEAVILY PROMOTED AS A GIFT SHOPPER'S PARADISE. THE FLOW OF TOURISTS THROUGH THIS SUGAR-COATED HAMLET IS NON-STOP AND, THEREFORE, FOR CYCLISTS, DOWNRIGHT UGLY. THE SPILLOVER IS HAVING SOME EFFECT ON THE NEIGHBORING TOWNS OF SANTA YNEZ AND LOS OLIVOS. YET, THE HILLS TO THE EAST OF LOS OLIVOS ARE SPARSELY SETTLED AND SELDOM TRAVELLED — YOU CAN BE THANKFUL FOR A FEW POTHOLES AND A LITTLE PATCHWORK PAVEMENT HERE FOR NO SELF-RESPECTING BMW / MERCEDES DRIVER WOULD BE CAUGHT IN SUCH A "ROUGH" NEIGHBORHOOD.

AFTER A GOOD 40-50 MILER IN THE HILLS TO THE EAST, RUMMAGE THROUGH YOUR GLOVE COMPARTMENT UNTIL YOU COME UP

DISTANCE –	40 MILES
DIRECTION –	COUNTERCLOCKWISE
HIGH POINT –	3,952'
LOW POINT –	830'
CAMPING –	FIGUEROA CAMP OR SUNSET VALLEY

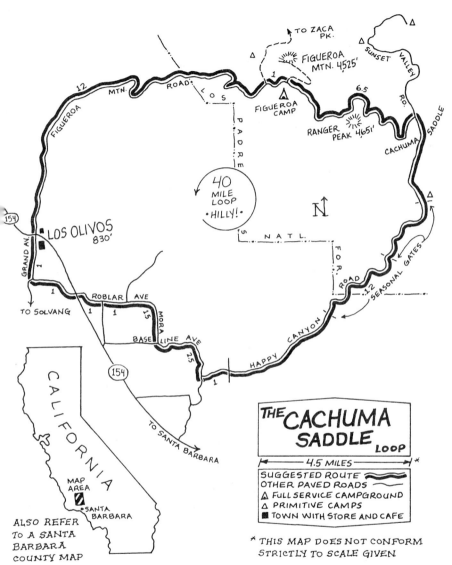

TO ZACA PK.

FIGUEROA MTN. 4525'

SUNSET VALLEY RD.

.12 FIGUEROA MTN. ROAD

LOS

FIGUEROA CAMP

6.5

RANGER PEAK 4651'

CACHUMA SADDLE

40 MILE LOOP •HILLY!

N

154

LOS OLIVOS 830'

PADRE

GRAND AV.

1

S NATL. FOR. ROAD .12

SEASONAL GATES

TO SOLVANG 1

ROBLAR AVE 1 1

.15

MORA AVE

BASE LINE AVE .25

154

1 HAPPY CANYON

TO SANTA BARBARA

CALIFORNIA

MAP AREA

Santa BARBARA

ALSO REFER
TO A SANTA
BARBARA
COUNTY MAP

THE CACHUMA SADDLE LOOP

4.5 MILES *

SUGGESTED ROUTE
OTHER PAVED ROADS
△ FULL SERVICE CAMPGROUND
△ PRIMITIVE CAMPS
■ TOWN WITH STORE AND CAFE

* THIS MAP DOES NOT CONFORM
STRICTLY TO SCALE GIVEN

WITH THE CLASSIC CYCLING BOOK WRITTEN BY LENA EMMERY AND
SALLY TAYLOR — GRAPE EXPEDITIONS IN CALIFORNIA. THERE
ARE SIX WINERIES WITHIN TEN MILES OF LOS OLIVOS THAT MIGHT
BE WORTH SOME RESEARCH. REMEMBER TO ELECT A DESIGNATED
DRIVER AND DON'T EVER DRIVE OR RIDE WHILE UNDER THE
INFLUENCE OF ALCOHOL.

5

POZO BASECAMP

IT'S UP TO YOU TO GET CREATIVE WITH THIS ONE. I'LL SUGGEST A POZO BASECAMP (AT LEAST PARK YOUR CAR NEAR THE FOREST SERVICE STATION HERE). IF YOU'RE GOING FOR BIG MILEAGE YOU SHOULD WEAR YOUR FAT TIRES AND TAKE IN ALL SIXTY-SIX MILES OF THE COMBINED LOOPS (INCLUDING THIRTEEN MILES OF DIRT).

BY MID-SUMMER THE NAKED HILLS HERE TURN A SERIOUS BROWN AND TEMPERATURES COMMONLY FLIRT WITH OR TOP THE ONE HUNDRED DEGREE MARK. EARLY SPRING IS BY FAR THE BEST TIME TO EXPLORE THESE HEADWATER CANYONS OF THE NORTH-FLOWING SALINAS RIVER.

WE ARRIVED IN POZO ON A MONDAY, PLANNING TO EXERCISE THE 66 MILE OPTION AND THEN TRY OUT THE TRACTOR SEATS IN THE POZO BAR (MADE FAMOUS BY ARTIST/AUTHOR EARL THOLLANDER) THAT EVENING.

AFTER A COOL WINTER RIDE THAT SAW US DIPPING IN AND OUT OF MINI-STORM SYSTEMS ALL MORNING, I COULD SEE THOSE DEEP, STEAMING CUPS OF HOT CHOCOLATE SITTING ON THE POZO BAR. WE WERE CRANKING EAST ALONG THE SANTA MARGARITA RESERVOIR AGAINST A SLIGHT HEADWIND WHILE TRYING TO IGNORE OUR FROZEN TOES.

THE LOOP COMPLETE, WE MOUNTED THE BIKES ATOP OUR '63 NOVA, PUT ON DRY SHIRTS AND LIMPED OVER TO THE POZO BAR FOR THAT THICK DECADENT HOT CHOCOLATE ... "CLOSED MONDAYS!" "HEY, I SWEAR THAT SIGN WASN'T UP THERE THIS MORNING."

DISTANCES –
20, 31 AND 20 MILE LOOPS

DIRECTION –
20 MI. LOOPS IN A COUNTERCLOCKWISE DIRECTION.
31 MI – CLOCKWISE.

HIGH POINT –
EL POZO SUMMIT 2,655'

LOW POINT –
BELOW DAM 1,295'

LODGING –
SANTA MARGARITA

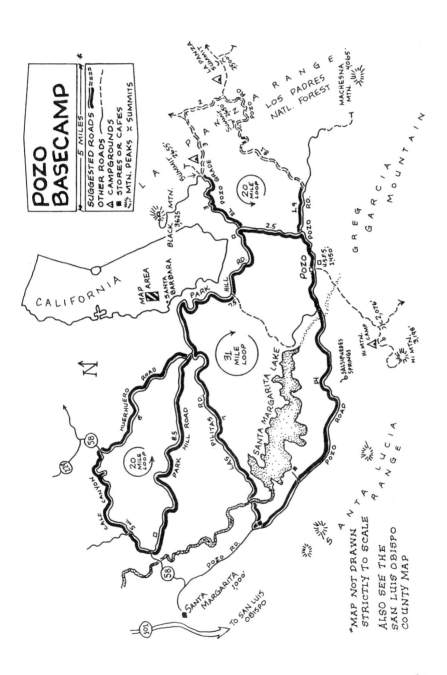

POZO
BASECAMP

5 MILES

Suggested Roads
Other Roads
Campgrounds
Stores or Cafes
Mtn. Peaks × Summits

CALIFORNIA

MAP AREA

SANTA BARBARA

BLACK MTN. 3625'

SUMMIT 2955'

LA PANZA SUMMIT 2500'

LA PANZA RANGE

LOS PADRES NATL. FOREST

POZA ANZA SUMMIT 3000'

EL POZO GRADE RD.

20 MILE LOOP

2.5

1.9

POZO RD.

POZO

U.S.F.S. 1450'

MACHESNA MTN. 4065'

GREGARIA GARCIA MOUNTAIN

N

PARK HILL RD.

HUERHUERO ROAD

PARK HILL ROAD

PILITAS RD.

LAS PILITAS RD.

31 MILE LOOP

SANTA MARGARITA LAKE

20 MILE LOOP

8.5

S. MTN.

CALF CANYON

58

229

SALSIPUEDES SPRINGS

HI MTN. CAMP 2,076'

HI MTN. 3,198'

POZO ROAD

SANTA LUCIA RANGE

POZO RD.

58

SANTA MARGARITA 1,000'

TO SAN LUIS OBISPO

101

*MAP NOT DRAWN STRICTLY TO SCALE

ALSO SEE THE SAN LUIS OBISPO COUNTY MAP

25

6

SAN LUIS OBISPO COUNTY

CAMBRIA - CAYUCOS

IT'S NO SECRET, MOUNTAIN LIFE IS OUR FAVORITE.
YET, WHEN THE SNOW GETS SLUSHY DURING LATE WINTER
NOTHING IS QUITE AS INVIGORATING AS A BIKE RIDE IN THE
COASTAL HILLS. THIS IS OUR FAVORITE CENTRAL COAST RIDE
AND A SPECTACULAR RIDE IT IS.

ONE WAY TO APPROACH THIS LOOP IS TO START IN
CAMBRIA (WHICH HAS SOME FINE BREAKFAST SPOTS AND AN
EXCELLENT BIKE SHOP). LET THAT PREDOMINENTLY DOWNCOAST
WIND BLOW YOU SOUTH ON HWY 1 (BIG SHOULDER) TOWARD
CAYUCOS — A GOOD WARM-UP SPIN FOR EARLY MORNING LEGS.
TAKE THE OLD HWY THROUGH DOWNTOWN CAYUCOS, MAKING
SURE YOU FILL THOSE WATER BOTTLES AND HAVE A FEW HI-ENERGY
BARS TUCKED IN YOUR JERSEY.

A FEW MILES SOUTH OF TOWN MAKE A LEFT ONTO
OLD CREEK ROAD — YOU'RE CLIMBING NOW!

BEYOND WHALE ROCK RESERVOIR THE ROAD
NARROWS AS IT CLIMBS THROUGH A CANYON OF ORANGE AND
AVOCADO TREES. YOU'LL TOP OUT AT 1400' BEFORE DROPPING
TO A CROSSING WITH A BUSY HWY
46. CONTINUE NORTH ON CYPRESS
MOUNTAIN ROAD — NOW YOU ARE
READY FOR SOME HEARTY CLIMB-
ING, (GEARS? A 45 INCH GEAR MAY
NOT GET YOU UP SOME OF THESE
WALLS).

ONCE YOU'VE ARRIVED
AT SKY RANCH (ELEV. 1862') IT'S TIME
TO CHANGE INTO YOUR D.T.U.'S
(DOWNHILL TRAINING UNITS). YOU
MIGHT ALSO WANT TO PULL OUT THE

DISTANCE —	45 MILES
DIRECTION —	COUNTERCLOCKWISE
HIGH POINT —	1862' - SKY RANCH
LOW POINT —	50' - CAYUCOS
CAMPING —	SAN SIMEON STATE BEACH
BIKE SHOP —	CAMBRIA BICYCLE OUTFITTERS — ASK FOR STEVE

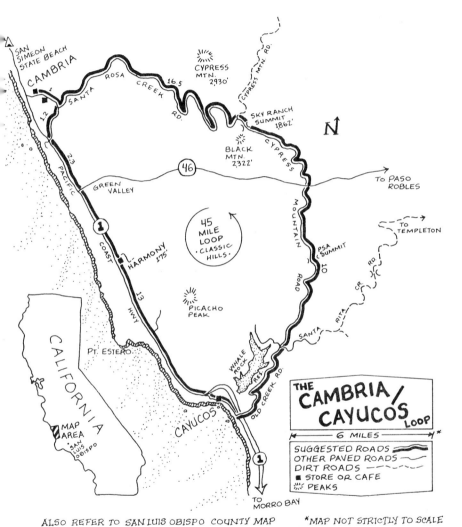

SAN SIMEON STATE BEACH

CAMBRIA

SANTA ROSA CREEK RD.

16.5

CYPRESS MTN. 2930'

CYPRESS MTN. RD.

SKY RANCH SUMMIT 1862'

1.2

2.3

N

BLACK MTN. 2322'

CYPRESS

(46)

TO PASO ROBLES

GREEN VALLEY

1

45 MILE LOOP · CLASSIC HILLS ·

MOUNTAIN

TO TEMPLETON

COAST

HARMONY ±75'

13

PSA SUMMIT

ROAD

HWY

PICACHO PEAK

PACIFIC

SANTA RITA CR. RD.

PT. ESTERO

CALIFORNIA

WHALE ROCK

RES.

MAP AREA

SAN LUIS OBISPO

CAYUCOS

OLD CREEK RD.

SANTA

THE CAMBRIA / CAYUCOS Loop

6 MILES

SUGGESTED ROADS
OTHER PAVED ROADS
DIRT ROADS — — —
■ STORE OR CAFE
☼ PEAKS

1

TO MORRO BAY

ALSO REFER TO SAN LUIS OBISPO COUNTY MAP   *MAP NOT STRICTLY TO SCALE

CAMERA — ON A CLEAR DAY THIS IS THE CLASSIC VISTA. THE SWITCHBACKS STACKED BELOW ARE LINED WITH LUPINE POPPYS AND COWS.

7

SAN LUIS OBISPO COUNTY

PEACHY CANYON LOOP

A BIKEE FRIEND IN SAN LUIS OBISPO HAS BEEN TELLING ME ABOUT THE GREAT RIDING IN HIS AREA FOR NEARLY A DECADE — "CAN'T BEAT THE RIDES HERE ... AND IT'S YEAR-ROUND RIDING." IT TURNS OUT THAT THE "GREAT RIDES" AREN'T ACTUALLY OUT OF SAN LUIS (THE TOWN IS A TRAFFIC NIGHTMARE) BUT ARE, RATHER, OUT OF TOWNS NEAR SAN LUIS OBISPO — SUCH AS: SANTA MARGARITA (RIDE NO. 5 POZO BASECAMP), CAYUCOS (RIDE NO. 6 CAYUCOS/CAMBRIA) AND PASO ROBLES (RIDE 7).

THE LOOP I'VE MAPPED HERE MAY SEEM SHORT MILEAGE - WISE; HOWEVER, DUE TO THE VARIETY OF TERRAIN (READ: HILLS) IT'LL MOST LIKELY ENTERTAIN YOU FOR OVER AN HOUR. IF YOU'RE ON FAT TIRES AND YOU LOVE LONG DISTANCE RIDING, AN EXCELLENT WAY TO STRETCH YOUR SADDLE TIME WOULD BE CONNECT WITH RIDE NO. 6 BY WAY OF CYPRESS MOUNTAIN RD. AND COMPLETING BOTH LOOPS FOR 95 MILES OF QUIET FUN AND OUTSTANDING SCENERY.

DIRECTION —
    COUNTERCLOCKWISE

DISTANCE —
    35 MILES

HIGH POINT —
    1,800' — ADELAIDA RD.

LOW POINT —
    730' — PASO ROBLES

AVERAGE SUMMER TEMPS —
    HOT!

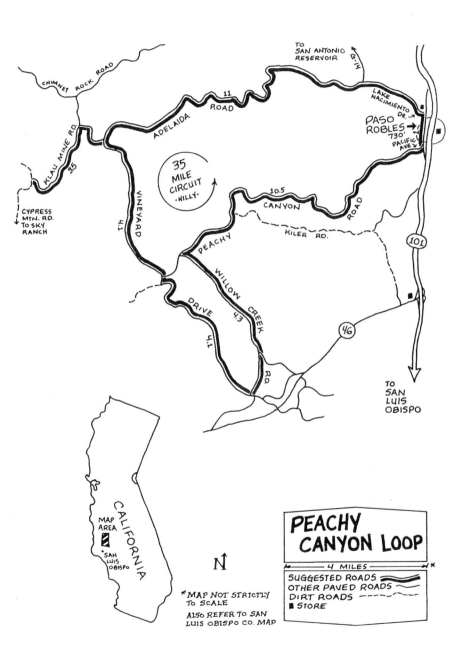

CHIMNEY ROCK ROAD

TO SAN ANTONIO RESERVOIR

G-14

ADELAIDA 11 ROAD

LAKE NACIMIENTO DR.

PASO ROBLES 730' PACIFIC AVE.

KLAU MINE RD. 35

CYPRESS MTN. RD. TO SKY RANCH

VINEYARD 4.1

35 MILE CIRCUIT ·HILLY·

10.5 CANYON ROAD

KILER RD.

PEACHY

WILLOW CREEK 4.3

DRIVE 4.1

RD.

101

46

TO SAN LUIS OBISPO

CALIFORNIA

MAP AREA

·SAN LUIS OBISPO

N

* MAP NOT STRICTLY TO SCALE

ALSO REFER TO SAN LUIS OBISPO CO. MAP

PEACHY CANYON LOOP

⊢— 4 MILES —⊣ *

SUGGESTED ROADS
OTHER PAVED ROADS
DIRT ROADS ---------
■ STORE

8

SAN LUIS OBISPO AND KERN COUNTIES

CHOLAME

CHOLAME – SOUNDS LIKE "SHAZAAM!"–A QUIET GREEN COUNTRY RIDE DURING LATE WINTER AND EARLY SPRING. WE STARTED THE LOOP BY CLIMBING A NEWLY PAVED PALO PRIETO CANYON ROAD WHICH ROLLS UP A SANDY WASH PEPPERED WITH COTTONWOODS AND OAKS.

DISTANCE - 38 MILES	
DIRECTION- EITHER WORKS WELL	
HIGH POINT – PALO PRIETO PASS 2,005'	
LOW POINT – 1,160' CHOLAME	
CAFE AND PARK – CHOLAME	

AT PALO PRIETO PASS YOU GET A LONG VIEW INTO CHOICE VALLEY... HORSE RANCHES, WINDMILLS AND WILDFLOWERS... AND A YOUNG COWBOY AT THE ROAD'S EDGE IN A '54 CHEVY PICK-UP, "HEY, WAIT A MINUTE." HE SNAPS, "WHERE ARE YOU FELLAS HEADED?" I TURNED AROUND AND RODE UP TO HIS OPEN WINDOW AS HE PINCHED THE BILL OF HIS HAT WITH HIS RIGHT THUMB AND INDEX FINGER, "DO YOU GUYS KNOW ABOUT THE ONE HUNDRED MILER THEY DO THROUGH HERE IN APRIL? THERE'S FELLAS ON THAT RIDE WHO SIT ON THEIR BUTTS ALL WINTER THEN COME OUT AND DO THE WHOLE DAMN RIDE!"

NOW WE'RE ROLLING BACK THROUGH CHOICE VALLEY, AN OLD SCHOOLHOUSE, A SMALL LAKE AND HORSES. WE TURN EAST OVER A SHORT, STEEP BLUFF PAST ANOTHER SCHOOLHOUSE AND A SIDE ROAD TO ANNETTE LOOKOUT — THE FLOWERS, PURPLES AND ORANGES, ARE ESPECIALLY INTENSE HERE.

AFTER A SHORT CLIMB NORTH WE'RE WHIZZING DOWN THE ORTEGA GRADE INTO SOME SERIOUS COW COUNTRY, NOT MUCH SHADE BUT THE SKY IS DEEP BLUE AND THE TEMPS ARE IN THE 70'S — THE SAN ANDREAS FAULT RUNS DEEP BELOW US, YET ON TWO WHEELS WE FEEL SECURE AND CARE-FREE.

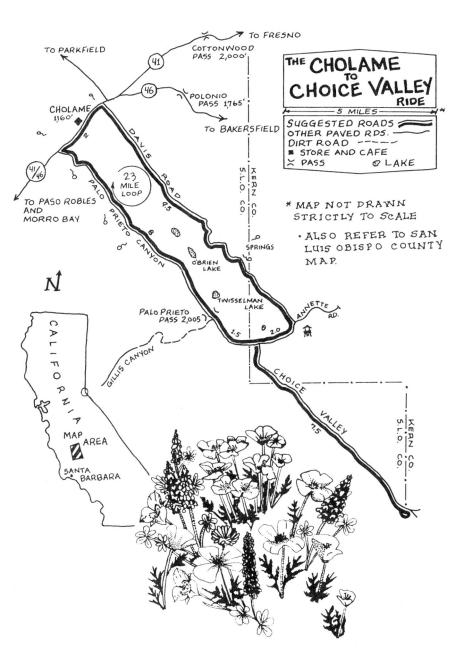

TO PARKFIELD

TO FRESNO

41

COTTONWOOD
PASS 2,000'

46

POLONIO PASS 1,765'

CHOLAME
1,160'

TO BAKERSFIELD

DAVIS ROAD

41/46

TO PASO ROBLES
AND
MORRO BAY

PALO PRIETO CANYON

23
MILE
LOOP

4.5

8

S.L.O. CO.   KERN CO.

THE CHOLAME TO CHOICE VALLEY RIDE

|← 5 MILES →| *

SUGGESTED ROADS
OTHER PAVED RDS.
DIRT ROAD ------
■ STORE AND CAFE
✕ PASS   ⊘ LAKE

* MAP NOT DRAWN
  STRICTLY TO SCALE

• ALSO REFER TO SAN
  LUIS OBISPO COUNTY
  MAP.

SPRINGS

OBRIEN
LAKE

N

TWISSELMAN
LAKE

PALO PRIETO
PASS 2,005'

ANNETTE
RD.

1.5   2.0

GILLIS CANYON

CALIFORNIA

MAP AREA

SANTA
BARBARA

CHOICE VALLEY

1.5

KERN CO.   S.L.O. CO.

31

9

VENTANA HILLCLIMBING

SMACK IN THE MIDDLE OF THE BIG SUR COAST, ONLY A HALF DOZEN MILES SOUTH OF SLEEPY LUCIA, YOU'LL FIND KIRK CREEK CAMPGROUND. ANOTHER MILE SOUTH AND TO THE EAST CLIMBS THE NACIMIENTO-FERGUSSON ROAD. THE NACIMIENTO-FERGUSSON ROAD STARTS A FEW DOZEN FEET ABOVE SEA LEVEL AND CLIMBS A TOWER OF

DISTANCE — 42 PAVED MILES
HIGH POINT — 3,106' – PAVED 5,103' – DIRT
LOW POINT — 48' – KIRK CREEK
CAUTION — AVOID THIS AREA DURING HUNTING SEASON.

SWITCHBACKS TO THE TOP OF THE COAST RANGE. ON A CLEAR DAY (TRY OCTOBER) THIS IS ONE SCENIC CLIMB.

AS YOU'VE NOTICED BY NOW MANY OF THE OUTINGS IN THIS BOOK INCLUDE ROADS FOR FAT TIRES AS WELL AS IDEAL ROADS FOR SKINNY TIRES. I FIRST RODE THIS CLIMB AS A SIDE TRIP ON A COAST TOUR IN THE EARLY 70'S WHEN MY TOURING PARTNER DECIDED SHE NEEDED A REST DAY AT KIRK CREEK CAMPGROUND.

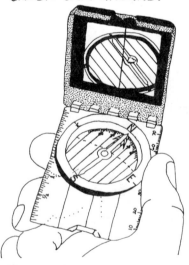

THIS ROAD IS OBVIOUSLY NOT ON MONTEREY COUNTY'S MONTHLY MAINTENANCE SCHEDULE — POT HOLES AND ROCKFALLS ARE QUITE COMMON. MAKE MENTAL NOTES OF SUCH HAZARDS AS YOU CLIMB AND PULL THEM DURING THE DESCENT. OVER THE TOP, THE ROAD IS IN BETTER SHAPE

THE CLIMB TO CONE PEAK IS STEEP (I LOVE THIS STUFF), BUT THE PAYOFF (TOP OF THE WORLD VIEW) IS OUTSTANDING.

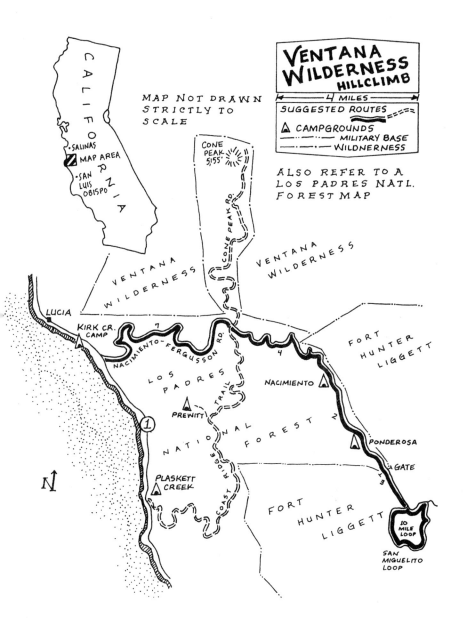

MAP NOT DRAWN
STRICTLY TO
SCALE

CALIFORNIA

• SALINAS
MAP AREA
• SAN
LUIS
OBISPO

VENTANA
WILDERNESS
HILLCLIMB

4 MILES
SUGGESTED ROUTES
⛺ CAMPGROUNDS
MILITARY BASE
WILDERNESS

ALSO REFER TO A
LOS PADRES NATL.
FOREST MAP

CONE PEAK
5,155'

CONE PEAK RD.

VENTANA
WILDERNESS

VENTANA
WILDERNESS

LUCIA

KIRK CR.
CAMP

NACIMIENTO-FERGUSSON RD.

7

4

FORT
HUNTER
LIGGETT

LOS
PADRES

NACIMIENTO ⛺

PREWITT ⛺

NATIONAL

COAST RIDGE TRAIL

FOREST

2

PONDEROSA ⛺

GATE

PLASKETT
CREEK ⛺

FORT

HUNTER

LIGGETT

3

10
MILE
LOOP

SAN
MIGUELITO
LOOP

N

10

EAGLE MOUNTAIN

DEFINITELY A QUIET LOOP! IMMEDIATELY UPON
LEAVING THE BUSY HIVE OF KING CITY
YOU'LL REALIZE YOU'RE IN FOR A PEACE-
FUL DAY IN THE SADDLE. THIS IS AN
IDEAL FEBRUARY, MARCH AND APRIL
LOOP... GREEN HILLS, WILDFLOWERS
AND RED TAIL HAWKS... GOOD ROAD
SURFACES HERE THAT ARE FRIENDLY
TO THE SKINNIEST OF TIRES.

DIRECTION —
  CLOCKWISE

DISTANCE — 40 MILES

HIGH POINT —
  1,769' ON G-13

LOW POINT —
  350' IN KING CITY

CAMPING —
  PINNACLES NATL.
  MONUMENT - 20mi.
  NORTH OF LOOP ON
  STATE HWY 25

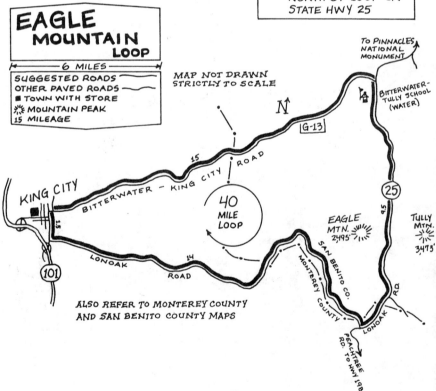

EAGLE
MOUNTAIN
LOOP

├─── 6 MILES ───┤

SUGGESTED ROADS
OTHER PAVED ROADS
■ TOWN WITH STORE
☀ MOUNTAIN PEAK
15 MILEAGE

MAP NOT DRAWN
STRICTLY TO SCALE

To PINNACLES
NATIONAL
MONUMENT

BITTERWATER-
TULLY SCHOOL
(WATER)

G-13

N

15

BITTERWATER — KING CITY ROAD

KING CITY

15

40
MILE
LOOP

25

9.5

EAGLE
MTN.
2,495'

TULLY
MTN.
3,473'

LONOAK

14

ROAD

101

MONTEREY COUNTY

SAN BENITO CO.

LONOAK RD.

PEACHTREE
RD. TO HWY 198

ALSO REFER TO MONTEREY COUNTY
AND SAN BENITO COUNTY MAPS

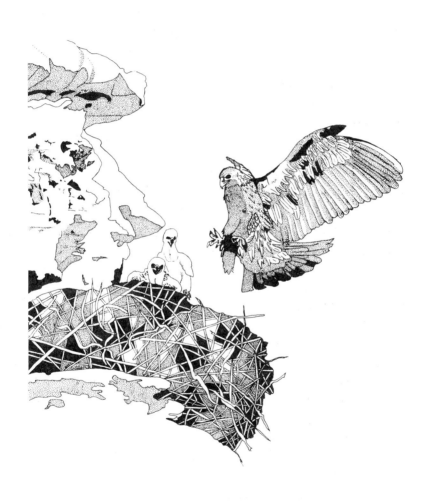

11

MARIN COUNTY

THE TOMALES LOOP

BAY AREA CYCLING EXPERTS CAN REMEMBER WHEN THE "HILLS BEYOND SUBURBIA" WERE IDEAL FOR CYCLING ANY DAY OF THE WEEK. THE HILLS OF MARIN COUNTY WERE AMONG THE BEST FOR TRAINING OR TOURING IN THE STATE. THIS MAY WELL BE THE LAST GREAT LOOP RIDE (GREAT: OUTSTANDING SCENERY COMBINED WITH INFREQUENT, HOWEVER PATIENT, MOTORISTS) IN ANY URBAN COUNTY IN THE STATE.

TOMALES PROVIDES THE ONLY GROCERY, REST-AURANT OR BED AND BREAKFAST ALONG THE RIDE. BE SURE TO PACK A LITTLE SNACK AND PLENTY OF WATER FOR FIFTY MILES OF CYCLING. YOU'LL BE ONLY A COUPLE OF MILES FROM PETALUMA AT THE HALFWAY POINT OF THE RIDE; HOWEVER, THIS IS NO LONGER A SLEEPY LITTLE CHICKEN-GROWING TOWN AND IS BEST AVOIDED BY THE TWO WHEEL TRAVELLER.

OUR APPROACH TO THIS ONE HAS BEEN TO CAMP ON DILLON BEACH, CLIMB THROUGH THE SMALL COMMUNITY OF DILLON BEACH (NO SERVICES), AND UP TO THE "ELEPHANT ROCKS". JUST BEYOND THE ROCKS WE TAKE A LEFT ON FRANKLIN SCHOOL RD. STICK WITH FRANKLIN SCHOOL AS IT ROLLS THROUGH AROMATIC EUCALYPTUS - LINED VALLEYS SPRINKLED WITH OLD WHITE HOMESTEADS SURROUNDED BY WEATHERED PICKET FENCES. KEEP AN EYE OUT FOR BIG COUNTRY DOGS. I STILL THINK THE BEST WAY TO DEAL WITH A COUNTRY DOG IS FOR YOU TO BARK A SHORT, SHARP COMMAND, "NO! GO HOME!" OR "GIT YOUR STICK!"

STARTING POINTS —
  TOMALES OR DILLON BEACH
DISTANCE —
  50 MILES
DIRECTION —
  CLOCKWISE
LODGING —
  BED + BREAKFAST IN TOMALES
CAMPING —
  DILLON BEACH
BIKE SHOP IN PETALUMA-
  BICYCLE FACTORY

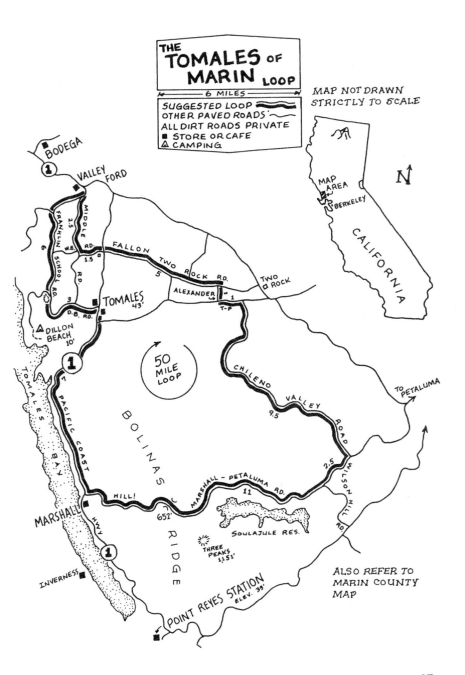

THE
TOMALES OF
MARIN LOOP

⊢———— 6 MILES ————⊣

MAP NOT DRAWN
STRICTLY TO SCALE

SUGGESTED LOOP ━━━━
OTHER PAVED ROADS ────
ALL DIRT ROADS PRIVATE
■ STORE OR CAFE
△ CAMPING

BODEGA
(1)
VALLEY FORD

FRANKLIN SCHOOL RD.
2.5
W.O
9
MIDDLE RD.
1.5
.8
FALLON
TWO ROCK RD.
5
TWO ROCK
ALEXANDER
1
T-P
.3
D.B. RD.
■ TOMALES
43'

△ DILLON
BEACH
10'

(1)

50
MILE
LOOP

CHILENO
VALLEY
ROAD
9.5

TO PETALUMA

BOLINAS

2.5

WILSON HILL RD.

PACIFIC COAST

TOMALES BAY

MARSHALL-PETALUMA RD.
11

HILL!
652'

SOULAJULE RES.

THREE
PEAKS
1151'

ALSO REFER TO
MARIN COUNTY
MAP

MARSHALL ■

HWY

(1)

RIDGE

INVERNESS ■

POINT REYES STATION
ELEV. 39'

MAP AREA
BERKELEY
N
CALIFORNIA

37

12

SOUTH SONOMA COAST

A SHORT LOOP BUT AN EXCELLENT WORKOUT. YOU MIGHT BEGIN THIS RIDE FROM A BED AND BREAKFAST IN BODEGA, A HOTEL ROOM IN BODEGA BAY, OR ONE OF THE CAMPGROUNDS ON THE BEACH. WE USUALLY OPT FOR ONE OF THE CAMPGROUNDS (DORAN PARK FEATURES HOT SHOWERS).

DISTANCE — 22 MILE LOOP
DIRECTION — EITHER
HIGH POINT — 1,006'
LOW POINT - SEA LEVEL
LODGING –
   HOTELS-BODEGA BAY
   CAMPING - SONOMA
   COAST STATE
   BEACHES
   • DORAN PARK
   • DUNCAN MILLS,
     GEORGE CASINIS

WES WILLIAMS OF SEBASTOPOL WAS MY MAIN TIPSTER ON THIS LOOP, "A GOOD FAT TIRE (FAT BOY) LOOP. WE USUALLY DO IT COUNTERCLOCKWISE FROM THE EAST END (OCCIDENTAL)." WHICH MEANS TRAVELLING DOWN COLEMAN VALLEY ROAD... CAUTION: IT IS OFTEN FOGGY HERE AND THE ROAD IS PATCHY AND FULL OF SURPRISES — LIVESTOCK, SLOW TRACTORS, POTHOLES AND RUBBER NECKERS IN VOLVOS.

LISA, COLBY (OUR LITTLE FISH), AND I DID IT CLOCK-WISE FROM BODEGA BAY. HWY 1 CAN GET A LITTLE TIGHT ON WEEKENDS SO GET AN EARLY START. CLIMBING COLEMAN VALLEY ROAD (WITH A BABY TRAILER) IS A TREAT, A GOOD WAY TO WARM-UP. THE FOG THINS NEAR THE TOP, THEN PRESTO!...BLUE SKY, EUCALYP TUS HEAVEN, GREEN GRASS HOMESTEADS.   JOY ROAD IS APTLY NAMED, BUT YOU MUST LOVE HILLS.

BODEGA, QUAINT YET STILL A LITTLE SPOOKY IF YOU REMEMBER THAT ALFRED HITCHCOCK'S THRILLER THE BIRDS WAS FILMED HERE. GREAT CAFES, A VICTORIAN BED AND BREAKFAST, A HANDFUL OF WELL-KEPT GARDENS AND A SURPRISING LACK OF NEW DEVELOPMENT MAKE BODEGA ESPECIALLY MEMORABLE.

BAY HILL ROAD IS ANOTHER SUDDEN CLIMB INTO THE EUCALYPTUS AND THEN ALONG THE CREST OF SHEEP RIDGE TO MT.

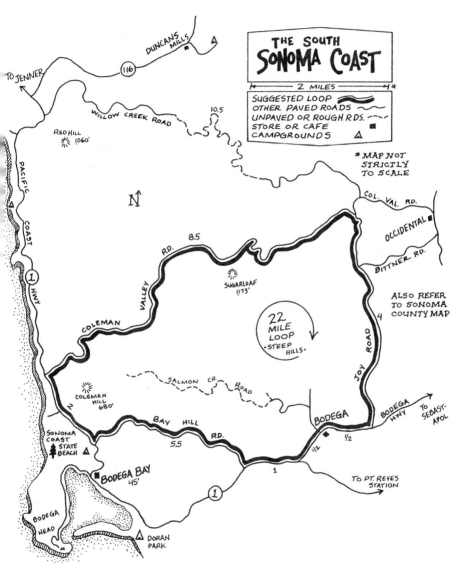

THE SOUTH
SONOMA COAST

|← 2 MILES →|*

SUGGESTED LOOP
OTHER PAVED ROADS
UNPAVED OR ROUGH RDS. ----
STORE OR CAFE ■
CAMPGROUNDS △

* MAP NOT
STRICTLY
TO SCALE

DUNCANS MILLS △

TO JENNER

(116)

WILLOW CREEK ROAD

10.5

RED HILL
1060'

PACIFIC COAST HWY

1

△

N↑

8.5

VALLEY RD.

COLEMAN

COLEMAN HILL 680'

SUGARLOAF 1173'

22 MILE LOOP · STEEP HILLS ·

SALMON CR. ROAD

BAY HILL RD.

5.5

SONOMA COAST STATE BEACH △

■ BODEGA BAY 45'

BODEGA HEAD

△ DORAN PARK

1

(1)

COL. VAL. RD.

OCCIDENTAL ■

BITTNER RD.

ALSO REFER TO SONOMA COUNTY MAP

JOY ROAD

4

BODEGA

■ 1/2

1/2

BODEGA HWY

TO SEBAST-APOL

TO PT. REYES STATION

ROSCOE, FOLLOWED BY A SUDDEN DROP TO HIGHWAY 1 AND THE
BUSY RESORT VILLAGE OF BODEGA BAY.

39

13
SONOMA COUNTY

NORTH SONOMA COAST

SONOMA COUNTY HAS BEEN A FAVORITE WITH US IN LATE FEBRUARY OR EARLY MARCH (THE SNOW IN THE HIGH COUNTRY STARTS TO GET A BIT SOGGY.) WE PACK UP THE OLD NOVA AND THROW THE ROAD BIKES ON TOP — ON THE OTHER HAND, FAT TIRES AND LOW GEARING MAY BE BEST ON THE TWO LOOPS DEPICTED HERE. THE ROADS HERE ARE STEEP AND UNPREDICTABLE DURING SPRING DUE TO MUD SLIDES AND ROCK FALLS; YOU NEVER KNOW WHAT TYPE OF SURFACE YOU'LL ENCOUNTER.

THE 25 MILE STEWART'S POINT / ANAPOLIS LOOP IS PROBABLY BEST BEGUN FROM SEA RANCH — PLENTY OF PARKING OPPORTUNITIES, A FEW PLACES FOR EATING AND ENJOYING A COLD DRAUGHT UPON YOUR RETURN, AND MOST IMPORTANTLY, A FEW MILES OF DOWNCOAST RIDING TO LOOSEN THE HAMS AND QUADS BEFORE TACKLING THE FORMIDABLE CLIMBS INLAND.

AFTER CROSSING THE RIDGE BETWEEN THE SOUTH FORK AND THE WHEATFIELD FORK OF THE GUALALA RIVER, YOU HAVE THE OPTION OF CLIMBING SIXTEEN MILES UP SKAGGS SPRINGS ROAD TO THE 1950' SUMMIT.

THE HOLLOW TREE GROCERY IN ANAPOLIS PROVIDES A TIMELY SNACK STOP BEFORE YOU RETURN TO THE COAST.

THE CAZADERO / PLANTATION LOOP IS EVEN MORE REMOTE AND SCENIC. THE CAZADERO INN IS THE PERFECT BASECAMP FOR THIS 40 MILE JAUNT (NO SERVICES ALONG THIS CIRCUIT).

DISTANCES —
25 AND 40 MILE LOOPS

DIRECTION —
COUNTERCLOCKWISE

HIGH POINTS —
25 MI. LOOP - 630'
40 MI. LOOP - 1625'

LOW POINTS —
25 MI. LOOP - SEA LEVEL
40 MI. LOOP - 117'

CAMPGROUNDS - SALT PT. AND DUNCANS MILLS

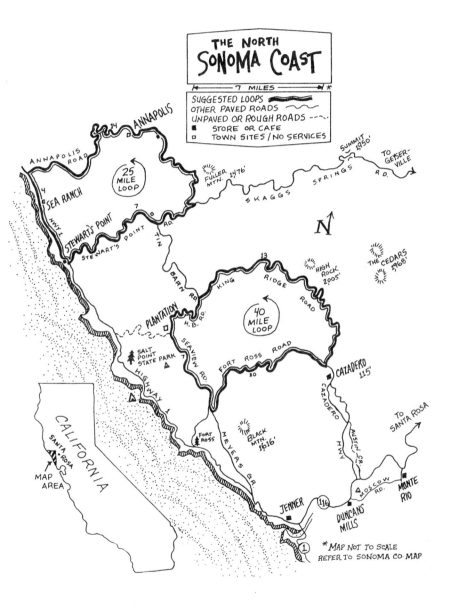

THE NORTH
SONOMA COAST

|← 7 MILES →| *

SUGGESTED LOOPS ▬▬▬▬▬
OTHER PAVED ROADS ─────
UNPAVED OR ROUGH ROADS ─ ─ ─
■ STORE OR CAFE
□ TOWN SITES / NO SERVICES

ANNAPOLIS

14

ANNAPOLIS ROAD

FULLER MTN. 1476'

SKAGGS SPRINGS RD.

SUMMIT 1950'

TO GEYSER-VILLE

25 MILE LOOP

SEA RANCH

HWY 1

STEWARTS POINT

4

7

STEWART'S POINT RD.

TIN BARN RD.

N↑

13

HIGH ROCK 2005'

THE CEDARS 3968'

KING RIDGE ROAD

40 MILE LOOP

PLANTATION

H.B. RD.

SEAVIEW RD.

7

SALT POINT STATE PARK

FORT ROSS ROAD

10

CAZADERO 115'

HIGHWAY 1

FORT ROSS

MEYERS GR.

BLACK MTN. 1616'

CAZADERO HWY

AUSTIN CR.

TO SANTA ROSA

CALIFORNIA

SANTA ROSA

MAP AREA

JENNER

116

MOSCOW RD.

DUNCANS MILLS

MONTE RIO

1

* MAP NOT TO SCALE
REFER TO SONOMA CO. MAP

14

MENDOCINO COUNTY
MENDOCINO COAST

HENDY WOODS STATE PARK— REDWOODS, HOT SHOWERS AND A BEAUTIFUL FRISBEE THROWING MEADOWS BEHIND CAMPING UNIT 57 – YOU COULDN'T ASK FOR A BETTER BASECAMP. AUTUMN MAY BE THE MAGIC TIME TO RIDE IN THIS AREA — RIPE APPLES AND OTHER

> DISTANCES – 40, 67 AND 8 mi.
> DIRECTION — ALL COUNTERCLOCKWISE
> HIGH POINT – 2,625' ON MOUNTAIN VIEW RD.
> LOW POINT — SEA LEVEL
> CAMPGROUNDS – VAN DAMME, PAUL M. DIMMICK, HENDY WOODS, MANCHESTER BCH.

TREATS AT FRUITSTANDS IN AND AROUND BOONVILLE... BLUE SKIES, FEW MOTORISTS AND UNCROWDED PARKS AND CAMPS, A GREAT TIME TO RIDE THESE QUIET COASTAL LANES.

THESE LOOPS EXPOSE YOU TO SOME HIGHWAY ONE TRAFFIC, WHICH DURING PEAK SEASON CAN BE A LITTLE HECTIC; HOWEVER, HWY ONE IS A WELL-ESTABLISHED CALIFORNIA BIKE ROUTE. YOU SHOULD HAVE SOME TWO WHEEL COMPANY OUT THERE AND MOTORISTS ARE QUITE ACCUSTOMED TO ALLOWING SPACE FOR CYCLISTS AT THE ROAD'S EDGE.

WE STARTED THE NORTH LOOP AT THE FLOOD GATE CAFE IN NAVARRO. WE PARKED IN AN OUT-OF-THE-WAY PLACE, DOWNED SOME STRONG COFFEE AND ASKED THE PROPRIETORS IF OUR CAR SITTING ON THE EDGE OF THEIR PARKING LOT FOR A COUPLE OF HOURS WOULD CAUSE A PROBLEM – YOU MUST PAY THIS COURTESY TO ANY MERCHANT YOU PARK NEAR.

IT WAS A QUICK DROP TO FLYNN CREEK RD. WHICH PROVIDED A PEACEFUL CLIMB TO COMPTCHE, A SURPRISING LITTLE VILLAGE WITH A POST OFFICE, A SMALL PART-TIME STORE AND A LOT OF BAREFOOT FOLKS IN LUSH GARDENS. ALBION ALSO HAS A LITTLE STORE AND A FEW CAFES WITH AN OCEAN VIEW.

ON THE 67 MILE LOOP, MOUNTAIN VIEW RD. IS A BIT LONLIER THAN MOST (MAY BE BEST ON FAT TIRES – SLIDES ARE COMMON.

To Mendocino

Van Damme State Pk.
Little Riv.

Airport Rd.
Comptche - Ukiah Rd.

Comptche 185'

To Ukiah

40 Mile Loop

Albion

Navarro Ridge

Flynn Creek

THE MENDOCINO COAST

9 MILES

SUGGESTED LOOPS
OTHER PAVED ROADS
SUGGESTED DIRT
■ STORE, CAFE OR FRUIT STAND
△ CAMPING   🌲 PARK

Cameron

Paul M. Dimmick Camp

Navarro 270'

MAP AREA   Ukiah

128

CALIFORNIA

1

Elk

Philo-Greenwood Rd.

67 Mile Loop

Hendy Woods State Pk.

Philo   8

Cold Springs Lookout 2700'

Highway

Boonville 400'

Manchester State Beach

Mountain View Rd

Summit Spring 2,016'

To Cloverdale

N

Point Arena 200'

(Many Summits) 26

To San Francisco

* MAP NOT STRICTLY TO SCALE
ALSO REFER TO MENDOCINO CO. MAP

43

15

HUMBOLDT COUNTY
UNKNOWN COAST

I FIRST MAPPED THIS
AREA IN THE LATE 70'S FOR A
SMALL PAMPHLET OF FAVORITE
BICYCLE RIDES IN FAR NORTHERN
CALIFORNIA. A LOT OF CYCLISTS
HAVE PASSED THROUGH HERE IN THE
LAST DOZEN YEARS WITH EVENTS
ORGANIZED BY CYCLISTS IN NEARBY
EUREKA AND ARCATA AS WELL AS
BY VARIOUS CLUBS IN THE SACRA-

DISTANCE — 100 MILES
HIGH POINT—
  PANTHER GAP 2,745'
LOW POINT—
  CAPETOWN
  AND THE BEACH 40'
BIKE SHOP—
  EUREKA AND ARCATA
CAMPING—
  HUMBOLDT STATE PARK
  A.W. WAY - HONEYDEW

MENTO VALLEY AND SAN FRANCISCO BAY AREAS. EVEN THOUGH
THE TWO WHEEL TRAFFIC HAS INCREASED OVER THE LAST
DECADE, THE MOTOR TRAFFIC IS ABOUT THE SAME.

THIS LOOP SERVES-UP AN AMAZING VARIETY OF
MICROCLIMES AND VEGETATION ZONES. KEEP YOUR EYES WIDE
OPEN BECAUSE THESE ROADS HAVE A WAY OF SERVING-UP
THEIR OWN SURPRISES — POT HOLES, ROCKS AND SAND ON THE
CORNERS. WE WERE IN THE SADDLES OF MOUNTAIN GOATS™
OUR LAST TIME AROUND AND WHAT A PLEASURE THAT WAS, A
DEEP WELL OF GEARS FOR THOSE 20+% GRADES AND THE
ULTIMATE IN STABILITY AS WE SKATED ACROSS PATCHES OF NEW-
LY GRAVELLED TARMAC.

IF YOU ARE INTO CAMPING, ESTABLISHING A BASE-
CAMP AT ALBEE CREEK IN HUMBOLDT STATE PARK IS A GREAT WAY
TO START — SET UP THE TENT, COOK SOME PASTA, DRINK A BEER
AND GET A GOOD NIGHT'S SLEEP. A COUNTERCLOCKWISE RIDE
WILL GIVE YOU A SLIGHT DOWNHILL AND A JUMP ON MORNING
TRAFFIC DOWN THE AVENUE OF THE GIANTS AND HWY 101.

IF YOU'RE LOOKING TO BE PAMPERED A BIT YOU CAN
RENT A VICTORIAN BED AND BREAKFAST SET-UP IN FERNDALE.

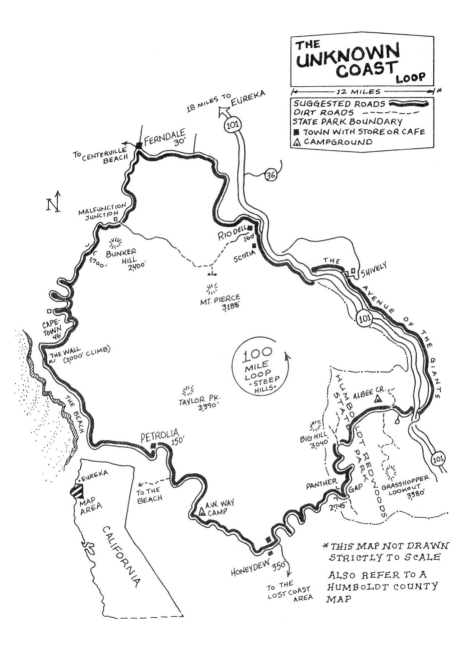

THE
UNKNOWN
COAST LOOP

|← 12 MILES →|*
SUGGESTED ROADS ▬▬▬▬
DIRT ROADS − − − − −
STATE PARK BOUNDARY
■ TOWN WITH STORE OR CAFE
△ CAMPGROUND

18 MILES TO EUREKA
101

FERNDALE 30'

To CENTERVILLE BEACH

N

36

MALFUNCTION JUNCTION

RIO DELL 160'

SCOTIA

BUNKER HILL 2400'
1700'

THE

SHIVELY

AVENUE OF THE GIANTS

MT. PIERCE 3,188'

CAPE-TOWN 46'

THE WALL (1000' CLIMB)

THE BEACH

101

100 MILE LOOP • STEEP HILLS.

TAYLOR PK. 3,390'

HUMBOLDT REDWOODS STATE PARK

ALBEE CR. △

BIG HILL 3,040'

GRASSHOPPER LOOKOUT 3,380'

101

PETROLIA 150'

EUREKA

MAP AREA

TO THE BEACH

CALIFORNIA

A.W. WAY CAMP

PANTHER GAP 2,745'

HONEYDEW 350'

TO THE LOST COAST AREA

* THIS MAP NOT DRAWN STRICTLY TO SCALE

ALSO REFER TO A HUMBOLDT COUNTY MAP

45

16

CALLAHAN·SCOTT VALLEY

A FEW MILES EAST, AND OVER A MILE BELOW THE MARBLE MOUNTAIN WILDERNESS, LIES THE SCOTT VALLEY. FIVE MILES WIDE AND NEARLY THIRTY MILES LONG, THE NUMEROUS BRANCHES OF THE SCOTT RIVER COLLECT HERE BEFORE SPILLING DOWN THE PRECIPITOUS SCOTT RIVER CANYON TO JOIN THE MIGHTY KLAMATH.

THIS IS, WITHOUT A DOUBT, THE EASIEST SIXTY MILE LOOP IN THE BOOK. SO AS NOT TO SEND ANY-ONE ON A HAZARDOUS OUTING THROUGH OVERSPRAYED AG LANDS, WE'VE SHIED AWAY FROM FLATLAND LOOPS IN THIS VOLUME. THIS IS ONE SPECIAL VALLEY AND UNLIKE THE SHASTA VALLEY TO THE EAST, CYCLING HERE IS NOT HAMPERED BY CYCLONIC WINDS.

THE U.S. ARMY CORPS OF ENGINEERS HAVE BEEN LICKING THEIR CHOPS OVER THE PROSPECT OF THROW-ING A DAM ACROSS THE HEAD OF THE SCOTT RIVER CANYON NEAR FT. JONES; THEREFORE, FILLING THE SCOTT VALLEY AND FORMING ONE OF THE LARGEST RESERVOIRS IN CALIF.

UNDERSTANDABLY, SCOTT VALLEY CITIZENS ARE AGAINST THE IDEA ... " THERE'S FIVE GENER-ATIONS OF BLOOD AND SWEAT LYING HERE AT THE BASE OF THE SALMON MOUNTAINS AND I'M ONE GUY THEY'RE GONNA HAVE TO DRAG OUT OF HERE WITH A CATERPILLAR TRACTOR IF THEY DECIDE TO FLOOD IT." PROTESTED LIFELONG RESIDENT, MICHAEL P. CALLAHAN.

DISTANCE — 60 MILES
DIRECTION — COUNTERCLOCKWISE
HIGH POINT — 3,210' CALLAHAN
LOW POINT — 2,650' QUARTZ VALLEY
CAMPING —
    U.S.F.S. SITES IN THE SCOTT RIVER CANYON
    PRIVATE CAMP AND COMMUNITY SWIMMING POOL IN ETNA

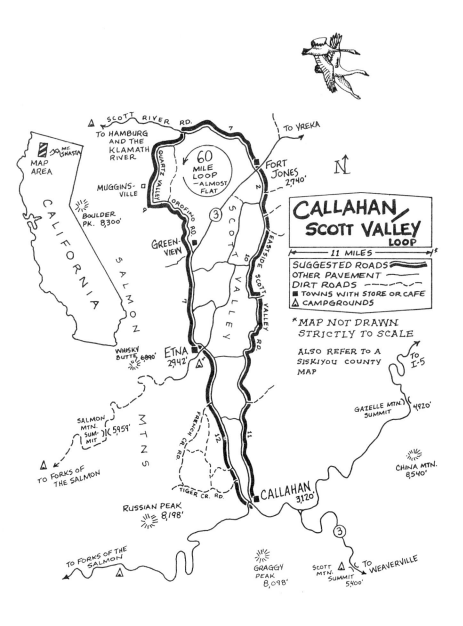

SCOTT RIVER RD.

7

TO VREKA

TO HAMBURG
AND THE
KLAMATH
RIVER

MT.
SHASTA

MAP
AREA

QUARTZ VALLEY

60
MILE
LOOP
—ALMOST
FLAT

FORT
JONES
2,740'

2

MUGGINS-
VILLE

BOULDER
PK. 8,300'

OROFINO RD.

3

C
A
L
I
F
O
R
N
I
A

S
A
L
M
O
N

GREEN-
VIEW

SCOTT

VALLEY

10

EASTSIDE SCOTT VALLEY RD.

N

CALLAHAN
SCOTT VALLEY
LOOP

|—— 11 MILES ——|

SUGGESTED ROADS
OTHER PAVEMENT
DIRT ROADS
■ TOWNS WITH STORE OR CAFE
△ CAMPGROUNDS

*MAP NOT DRAWN
STRICTLY TO SCALE

ALSO REFER TO A
SISKIYOU COUNTY
MAP

TO
I-5

WHISKY
BUTTE 6,890'

ETNA
2,942'

△

M
T
N
S

SALMON
MTN.
SUM-
MIT)(5,959'

FRENCH CR. RD.

12

11

GAZELLE MTN.
SUMMIT

4,920'

CHINA MTN.
8,540'

△

TO FORKS OF
THE SALMON

TIGER CR. RD.

CALLAHAN
3,120'

3

RUSSIAN PEAK
8,198'

TO FORKS OF THE
SALMON

△

GRAGGY
PEAK
8,098'

SCOTT
MTN.
SUMMIT
5,400'

△

TO WEAVERVILLE

FOOTHILL RIDES

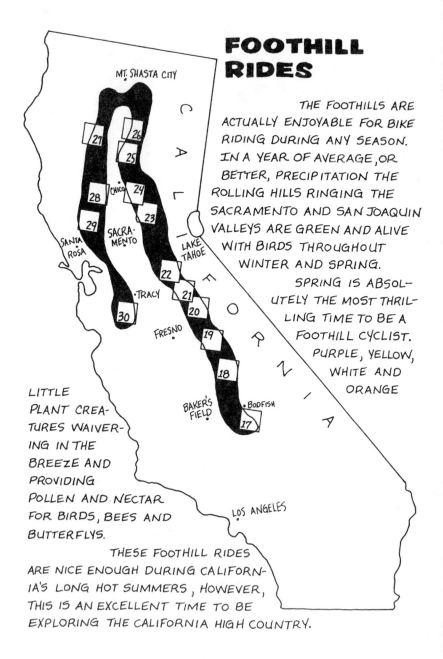

THE FOOTHILLS ARE ACTUALLY ENJOYABLE FOR BIKE RIDING DURING ANY SEASON. IN A YEAR OF AVERAGE, OR BETTER, PRECIPITATION THE ROLLING HILLS RINGING THE SACRAMENTO AND SAN JOAQUIN VALLEYS ARE GREEN AND ALIVE WITH BIRDS THROUGHOUT WINTER AND SPRING.

SPRING IS ABSOLUTELY THE MOST THRILLING TIME TO BE A FOOTHILL CYCLIST. PURPLE, YELLOW, WHITE AND ORANGE LITTLE PLANT CREATURES WAIVERING IN THE BREEZE AND PROVIDING POLLEN AND NECTAR FOR BIRDS, BEES AND BUTTERFLYS.

THESE FOOTHILL RIDES ARE NICE ENOUGH DURING CALIFORNIA'S LONG HOT SUMMERS, HOWEVER, THIS IS AN EXCELLENT TIME TO BE EXPLORING THE CALIFORNIA HIGH COUNTRY.

48

17

KERN COUNTY
SOUTH OF BODFISH

IN THE EARLY SEVENTIES I SET UP CAMP FOR THE WINTER IN A LITTLE KNOWN, SELDOM VISITED, SIDE CANYON OF THE KERN RIVER IN A BERG CALLED "FLUME BODFISH". I RENTED A CABIN, STARTED A LITTLE GARDEN AND MADE FRIENDS WITH A GROUP OF KERN CANYON COUNTRY EXPLORERS. WE FOUND RIDGES TO SKI, TAILINGS TO PAN, HOT SPRINGS TO SOAK IN, SLABS AND APRONS TO CLIMB, LIMESTONE HOLES TO SQUEEZE INTO, PEAKS TO BAG AND, AS IT TURNED OUT – MOST IMPORTANTLY, ROADS TO BICYCLE.

DISTANCES –	
ALL PAVEMENT	75 MILES
DIRECTION –	
COUNTERCLOCKWISE	
HIGH POINT –	
4,010' – HOOPER HILL	
LOW POINT –	
1,300' – CALIENTE	
CAMPGROUNDS –	
HOBO CAMP AND SADDLE SPRINGS AND VARIOUS SITES AROUND LAKE ISABELLA	

THE LOCALS AT THE TIME PREFERRED TO CYCLE THE LOOP AROUND THE LAKE – A 45 MILE MIXTURE OF WIND, TRAFFIC, ROLLING HILLS AND GOOD VIEWS OF THE HIGH COUNTRY NORTH OF LAKE ISABELLA. I WAS MORE INTERESTED IN THE "OUTBACK" TRACKS AND ROADS, (THIS HAS BEEN THE PATTERN THROUGHOUT MY LIFE... MY MOTHER WOULD SET ME IN THE SANDBOX IN OUR SPACIOUS FENCED BACKYARD AND MINUTES LATER I'D FIND A LOOSE BOARD IN THE FENCE, CRAWL THROUGH AND BEGIN MAPPING THE NEIGHBOR'S BACKYARD – IT WAS WILDER THAN OURS, OVERGROWN WITH VINES AND CHOKED WITH TALL GRASS AND UNTAMED WILLOW.)

THE ROADS BEHIND BODFISH (SOUTH) WILL SURPRISE YOU. THEY'RE QUIET, BORDERED BY GREENERY (DURING WINTER AND SPRING) AND LEAD TO NARY A CONDO DEVELOPMENT OR SUBDIVISION.

RIDING SOUTH FROM BODFISH YOU FIRST BREAK

ABOVE A WAVE OF MOBILE HOMES THAT COMPRISE THE
MAJORITY OF THE RESIDENCES IN BODFISH. IMMEDIATELY
CLIMBING A SERIES OF SWITCHBACKS TO THE EAST
SHOULDER OF HOOPER HILL BEFORE DESCENDING TO
HAVILAH AND ON INTO THE WALKER BASIN.

SIX MILES BEYOND THE SUMMIT YOU'LL SEE A
SEQUOIA NATIONAL FOREST RANGER STATION ON YOUR
LEFT (CHECK YOUR WATER SUPPLY HERE), CONTINUE RIDING
SOUTH ON THE BODFISH-CALIENTE ROAD. AT APPROXIMATELY
THE SIXTEEN MILE POINT YOU BEGIN CLIMBING WHAT LOCAL'S
CALL "THE LION'S TRAIL" — AN INTERESTING ASCENT
THROUGH BRIGHT GREEN OAKS AND SHOWY WILDFLOWERS
IN EARLY MARCH.

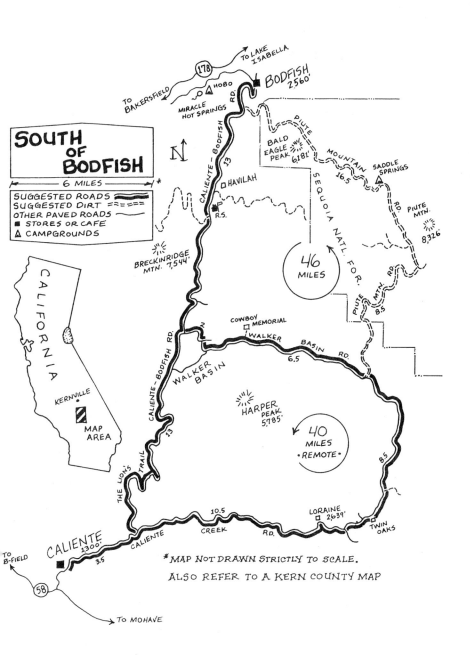

SOUTH OF BODFISH

├─ 6 MILES ─┤ *

SUGGESTED ROADS	▬▬▬▬
SUGGESTED DIRT	═══
OTHER PAVED ROADS	═══
■ STORES OR CAFE	
△ CAMPGROUNDS	

N↑

TO LAKE ISABELLA

178

TO BAKERSFIELD

○ △ HOBO
MIRACLE HOT SPRINGS

■ BODFISH 2,560'

BALD EAGLE PEAK 6,181'

PIUTE MOUNTAIN 16.5

SADDLE SPRINGS △

PIUTE MTN. 8,326'

CALIENTE – BODFISH RD.

13

□ HAVILAH

■ R.S.

SEQUOIA NATL. FOR.

BRECKINRIDGE MTN. 7,544'

46 MILES

PIUTE MTN. RD. 8.5

CALIFORNIA

KERNVILLE ●

MAP AREA

CALIENTE – BODFISH RD.

2

COWBOY MEMORIAL □
▮ WALKER

WALKER BASIN RD.

6.5

WALKER BASIN

HARPER PEAK 5,785'

40 MILES • REMOTE •

13

THE LION'S TRAIL

8.5

10.5

CALIENTE

CREEK

RD.

LORAINE □ 2,639'

TWIN OAKS

TO B-FIELD

CALIENTE 1,300'

■

3.5

58

TO MOHAVE

* MAP NOT DRAWN STRICTLY TO SCALE.

ALSO REFER TO A KERN COUNTY MAP

51

18

TULARE AND KERN COUNTIES

CALIFORNIA HOT SPRINGS

THE OBVIOUS PLACE TO START THIS RIDE IS AT THE CALIFORNIA HOT SPRINGS RESORT, WHERE THERE ARE TUBS FOR RENT, BREAKFAST IS SERVED AND A PARKED CAR WON'T BE BOTHERED. IF YOU PREFER CAMPING — LEAVIS FLAT, A U.S. FOREST SERVICE CAMPGROUND, IS NEARBY.

HEAT CAN BE A BIG FACTOR ON THIS LOOP. IF YOU'RE ATTEMPTING THIS 88 MILE LOOP DURING THE SUMMER OR EARLY FALL YOU SHOULD PLAN TO GET AN EARLY START AND ROLL DOWN M-56 TO FOUNTAIN SPRINGS AS EARLY AS POSSIBLE. TAKING THE OLD STAGE ROAD (M-109) SOUTH TOWARD WHITE RIVER YOU BEGIN A FORTY MILE CLIMB TO 7,280' PORTUGUESE PASS.

THE FIRST TIME LISA AND I RODE THE HIGH-COUNTRY PORTION OF THIS LOOP IT WAS MID-NOVEMBER AND A FEW DAYS AFTER THE FIRST BIG WINTER STORM. A FRIEND IN KERNVILLE TOLD US THE ROAD WAS CLEAR AND PAVED—"I'M ALMOST POSITIVE." WE WERE RETURNING TO NORTHERN CALIFORNIA FROM A TWO MONTH JOURNEY THROUGH COLORADO, NEW MEXICO, ARIZONA AND SOUTHERN CAL, SO THE PROSPECT OF SNOW, ICE AND POSSIBLE GAPS IN PAVED ROUTES DIDN'T PHASE US. IT TURNED OUT TO BE COMPLETELY PAVED AND ONLY A LITTLE ICY.

AS WITH MOST OF THE LOOPS IN THIS BOOK THE DISTANCE BETWEEN STORES AND EATERIES IS GREAT, SO BE SURE TO PACK SNACKS AND PLENTY OF WATER.

DISTANCE — 88 MILES

DIRECTION —
COUNTERCLOCKWISE

HIGH POINT —
PORTUGUESE PASS
7,280'

LOW POINT —
FOUNTAIN SPRINGS
800'

CAMPGROUNDS —
LEAVIS FLAT, WHITE
RIVER, PANORAMA

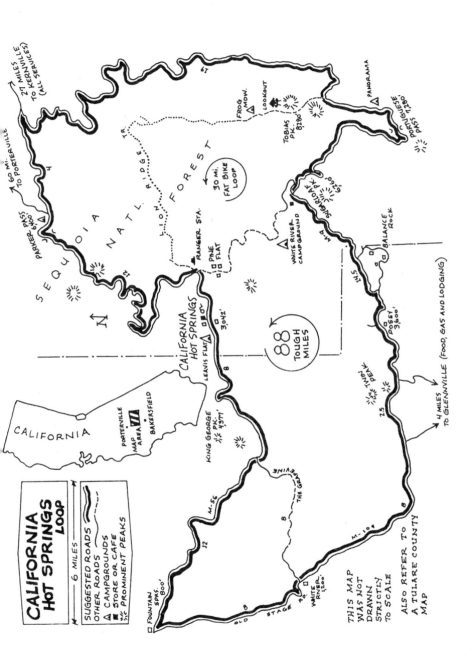

CALIFORNIA
HOT SPRINGS Loop

6 MILES

SUGGESTED ROADS
OTHER ROADS
△ CAMPGROUNDS
■ STORE OR CAFE
☀ PROMINENT PEAKS

CALIFORNIA

PORTERVILLE
MAP
AREA
BAKERSFIELD

SEQUOIA NATL. FOREST

LION RIDGE TR.

30 Mi.
FAT BIKE
LOOP

RANGER STA.

PINE FLAT

CALIFORNIA HOT SPRINGS

LEWIS FLAT 3,042'

88
TOUGH
MILES

↗ 27 MILES
TO KERNVILLE
(ALL SERVICES)

↗ 60 MILES
TO PORTERVILLE

PARKER PASS 7,400'

FROG MDW.

LOOKOUT

TOBIAS PK. 8,290'

PANORAMA

PORTUGUESE PASS 7,280'

WHITE RIVER CAMPGROUND

SHARKLOAF 6,260'

BALANCE ROCK

14.5

POSEY 3,600

TWIN PEAK

2.5

4 MILES
TO GLENNVILLE (FOOD, GAS AND LODGING)

KING GEORGE PK. 4,577'

M. 56

12

FOUNTAIN SPRS. 800'

THE GRAPEVINE

8

8

M. 104

WHITE RIVER 1,200'

OLD STAGE RD.

8

THIS MAP
WAS NOT
DRAWN
STRICTLY
TO SCALE

ALSO REFER TO
A TULARE COUNTY
MAP

N

53

19

FRESNO AND TULARE COUNTIES

THE KINGS HILLS

KINGS CANYON NATL. PARK HAS LONG BEEN MY FAVORITE BACKPACKING PARK IN THE WEST. AS A RESIDENT OF FRESNO DURING THE EARLY SEVENTIES, IT DIDN'T TAKE ME LONG TO FIGURE OUT THAT THE HILLS AND HIGH COUNTRY TO THE EAST WERE CENTRAL CALIFORNIA'S HEAVENLY HAUNTS.

I HAD AN OLD MERCURY METEOR — NOT A GREAT CLIMBER, AT 4,000 FEET THE TRANSMISSION FLUID WOULD OVERHEAT AND SOMETIMES CATCH FIRE.

MY MOTOBECANE GRAN JUBILEÉ ON THE OTHER HAND STAYED COOL ALL THE WAY TO 9,000'. I LOVED THESE HILLS — THIS IS WHERE I LEARNED TO BE TOUGH IN THE SADDLE, WHERE I LEARNED THAT ENDURING SOME LEG AND LUNG PAIN HAD ITS REWARDS.

AS A RULE, ON A CLEAR WINTER'S DAY, THE ROADS HERE ARE FREE OF SNOW UP TO AN ELEVATION NEAR 5,000' — 500' ABOVE THE HIGHEST POINT MAPPED HERE.

DISTANCES — 63, 19 OR 82 mi.

DIRECTION — ALL CLOCKWISE

HIGH POINT — 4,500' ESHOM CREEK

LOW POINT — 445'

CAMPING — ESHOM CR. OR TEN MILES TO SUNSET, AZALEA AND CRYSTAL SPRINGS CAMPGROUNDS IN KINGS CANYON NATIONAL PARK, TEN MILES ABOVE PINEHURST, WEATHER PERMITTING.

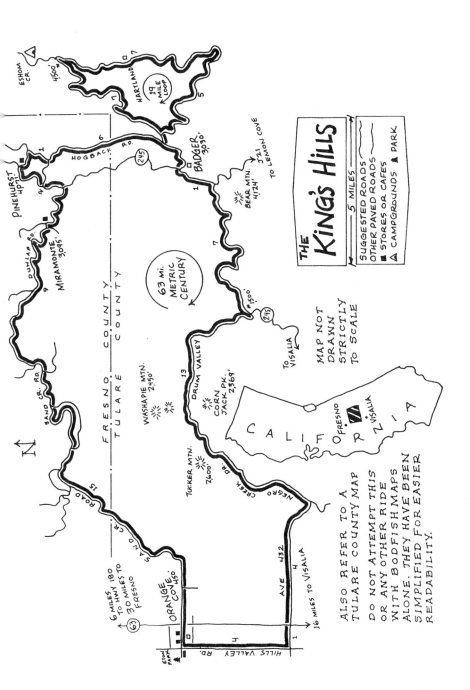

THE **King's Hills**

5 MILES

SUGGESTED ROADS
OTHER PAVED ROADS
STORES OR CAFES ■
CAMPGROUNDS ⛺ PARK ▲

MAP NOT
DRAWN
STRICTLY
TO SCALE

ESHOM CR. ▲
4500'

HARTLAND ☐ 7

19 MILE LOOP

HOGBACK RD.

PINEHURST 4001' ■

DUNLAP RD.

MIRAMONTE 3,045' ■

FRESNO COUNTY
TULARE COUNTY

SAND CR. RD.

245

BADGER 3,030' ■

BEAR MTN. 4,124'

J21 TO LEMON COVE

63 mi. METRIC CENTURY

1500'

245

TO VISALIA

WASHAPIE MTN. 2,450'

DRUM VALLEY 13

CORN JACK PK. 2,369'

TUCKER MTN. 2,600'

NEGRO CREEK DR.

CALIFORNIA
○ FRESNO
■ VISALIA

ROAD 15

SAND CR. ROAD

6 MILES TO HWY 180
30 MILES TO FRESNO

63 ORANGE COVE 450'

ETON PARK ▲

HILLS VALLEY RD.

AVE 432

16 MILES TO VISALIA

N ⬆

ALSO REFER TO A
TULARE COUNTY MAP

DO NOT ATTEMPT THIS
OR ANY OTHER RIDE
WITH BODFISH MAPS
ALONE. THEY HAVE BEEN
SIMPLIFIED FOR EASIER
READABILITY.

55

20

YOSEMITE FOOTHILLS

ON ANY LONG LOOP WHERE THERE ARE ONLY A COUPLE OF TOWNS TO BE ENCOUNTERED IN ROUTE, IT'S NICE TO POSITION YOUR BASECAMP IN A THIRD LOCATION.

DISTANCE - 88 MILES
DIRECTION - CLOCKWISE
HIGHPOINT - 5,525' CRANE MEADOW
LOWPOINT - 1056' WARD'S FERRY
LODGING - GROVELAND, SONORA AND YOSEMITE VALLEY
CAMPGROUND - CHERRY LK.

IN THIS CASE I SUGGEST CHERRY LAKE CAMPGROUND (IN THE NORTHEAST CORNER OF THIS MAP), AT 4,700' IT'S NEAR THE HIGH POINT OF THE JOURNEY AND YOU'LL GET SOME IDEA OF WHAT THE SNOW CONDITIONS ON THE ROAD ARE BEFORE EMBARKING ON YOUR LOOP... IN FACT, DRIVING UP COTTONWOOD ROAD FROM TUOLUMNE WILL HELP YOU RECONNOITER THIS MOST UNPREDICTABLE SECTION OF THE ROUTE.

NORMALLY THE RIDING SEASON HERE IS FROM MAY 1ST THROUGH DECEMBER 1ST; HOWEVER, THE LOOKOUT TOWER CLIMBS (DUCKWALL AND WOOD'S RIDGE) MAY BE OPEN FOR A SHORTER PERIOD... SAY, FROM JUNE 1ST THROUGH OCTOBER 31ST. THE WILDFLOWER DISPLAYS ARE OUTSTANDING IN MARCH AND APRIL ON THE WESTERN PORTION OF THIS LOOP (BELOW 3,000'). UNLESS IT'S BEEN A DRY WINTER, THE EASTERN HALF OF THE LOOP MAY STILL BE CLOGGED WITH SNOW.

LATE SUMMER FIRES WERE A COMMON OCCURANCE HERE DURING THE EIGHTIES, TAKE CARE TO DOUSE YOUR CAMPFIRES (DEAD OUT!) BEFORE LEAVING CAMP.

WARD'S FERRY ROAD, NORTH OF GROVELAND, IS A ONE LANE PAVED ROUTE SPRINKLED WITH HAZARDS — ROCKFALLS, POT HOLES AND 4WDRIVE FISHER PEOPLE WHO KEEP ONE EYE ON THE ROAD AND ONE ON THE RIVER.

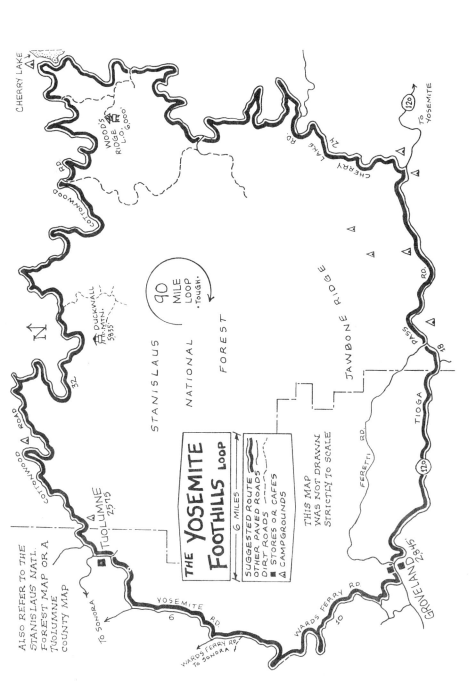

CHERRY LAKE

WOOD'S RIDGE L.O. 6,000'

COTTONWOOD RD.

DUCKWALL MTN. 5835'

32

COTTONWOOD ROAD

TUOLUMNE 2515

ALSO REFER TO THE STANISLAUS NAT'L. FOREST MAP OR A TUOLUMNE COUNTY MAP

N

STANISLAUS NATIONAL FOREST

90 MILE LOOP *TOUGH.

JAWBONE RIDGE

CHERRY LAKE RD.

24

120 TO YOSEMITE

PASS

81

TIOGA

FERETTI RD.

120

THE YOSEMITE Foothills LOOP

6 MILES

SUGGESTED ROUTE
OTHER PAVED ROADS
DIRT ROADS
■ STORES OR CAFES
△ CAMPGROUNDS

THIS MAP WAS NOT DRAWN STRICTLY TO SCALE

YOSEMITE RD.

6

TO SONORA

WARDS FERRY RD. TO SONORA

WARDS FERRY RD.

10

GROVELAND 2845

57

21
GOLD COUNTRY LOOPS

WE PARKED IN MURPHY'S, A SMALL VILLAGE NINE MILES ABOVE ANGEL'S CAMP JUST OFF HIGHWAY 4. IT'S MID-NOVEMBER — THE CAR'S WINDSHIELD IS FOGGING-UP WHILE I WRITE; WE FOUND THE ULTIMATE MOTHER LODE CENTURY TODAY (BROKEN DOWN HERE INTO TWO FORTY-PLUS MILE LOOPS). THIS IS NOT OUR FIRST TIME RIDING IN THESE HILLS, BUT TODAY WE PUT A COUPLE OF FAVORITE LOOPS TOGETHER AND "VOILA!"

IT STARTED WITH US CLIMBING NORTH OUT OF 2,170' MURPHY'S ON SAN DOMINGO STREET — WITHIN A MILE IT BECOMES SHEEP RANCH ROAD ... LEADING INTO THE MOTHER LODE OUTBACK; THIS RIDE TRAVERSES THE CANYONS AND RIDGES THAT STAND BETWEEN THE STANISLAUS AND MOKELUMNE RIVERS. ELEVATIONS RANGE BETWEEN 1,000 AND 3,000 FEET DURING THE RIDING OF THESE LOOPS, YET YOUR TOTAL ELEVATION GAIN MAY EXCEED 10,000' — MAKING FOR A FULL AND SATISFYING DAY IN (AND OUT OF) THE SADDLE.

THE MOTHER LODE IS BEING DEVELOPED AT A FRENETIC PACE. THOUSANDS OF URBANITES AND FLATLANDERS HAVE DISCOVERED THE ADVANTAGES OF LIVING ON THE WEST SLOPE ABOVE THE FOG AND THE AGRICULTURAL SMOG.

I DIDN'T FIND ANY HISTORICAL ACCOUNT ON THE NAMING OF JESUS MARIA ROAD; HOWEVER, YOU WILL BETTER UNDERSTAND THE ORIGIN OF THE NAME BY REPEATING IT SEVERAL TIMES AS YOU ASCEND (THE PERFECT HILLCLIMBING MANTRA).

DISTANCES — 49 AND 40 MILES, CONNECT FOR A 97 MILE LOOP

DIRECTION — COUNTERCLOCKWISE

HIGH POINT — 2,950' ON SHEEP RANCH ROAD

LOW POINT — 1,105' NEAR SAN ANDREAS

CAMPING — CALAVERAS BIG TREES STATE PK. 15 MILES ABOVE MURPHY'S

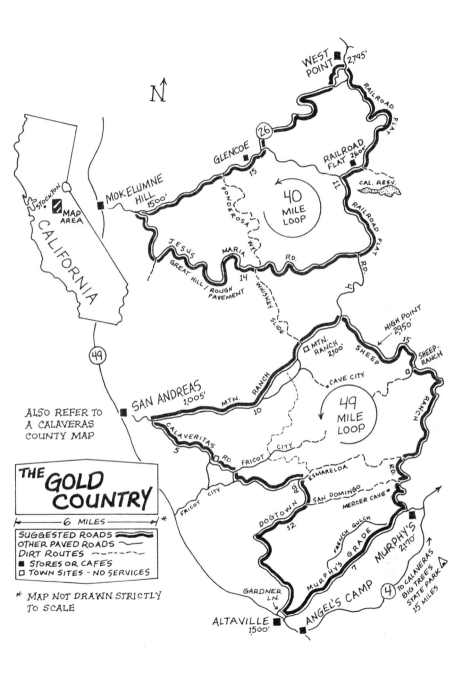

N

WEST POINT 2,795'

RAILROAD FLAT

26

GLENCOE

RAILROAD FLAT 2600'

CAL. RESV.

MOKELUMNE HILL 1500'

40 MILE LOOP

PONDEROSA WY.

RAILROAD FLAT RD.

JESUS MARIA RD.

GREAT HILL / ROUGH PAVEMENT

14

WHISKEY SLIDE

MTN. RANCH 2,100'

HIGH POINT 2950'

SHEEP RANCH

SHEEP RANCH

CAVE CITY

49 MILE LOOP

SAN ANDREAS 1,005'

MTN. RANCH RD.

10

ALSO REFER TO A CALAVERAS COUNTY MAP

CALAVERITAS

5

RD. FRICOT CITY

FRICOT CITY

ESMARELDA

SAN DOMINGO

MERCER CAVE

RD.

49

DOGTOWN

12

FRENCH GULCH

MURPHY'S 2,170'

THE GOLD COUNTRY

6 MILES

SUGGESTED ROADS
OTHER PAVED ROADS
DIRT ROUTES
■ STORES OR CAFES
□ TOWN SITES - NO SERVICES

MURPHY'S GRADE

7

ANGEL'S CAMP

4

TO CALAVERAS BIG TREES STATE PARK 15 MILES

* MAP NOT DRAWN STRICTLY TO SCALE

GARDNER LN.

ALTAVILLE 1,500'

STOCKTON

CALIFORNIA

MAP AREA

49

59

22

VOLCANO COUNTRY

FOR THE VERY REASON THAT IT'S NAMED VOLCANO THIS IS ONE OUTSTANDING BASECAMP FOR ONE WHO LOVES CHALLENGING CLIMBS ON QUIET ROADWAYS. THERE IS A SINGLE DESCENDING "SPILLWAY ROAD" OUT OF THE CRATER — THE SUTTER CREEK / VOLCANO ROAD, A NINE HUNDRED FOOT DROP TO HWY 49 AND HISTORIC SUTTER CREEK.

> **DISTANCES** — 25 AND 30 MILE LOOPS
> **DIRECTION** — COUNTERCLOCKWISE
> **HIGH POINT** — 3340'
> **LOW POINT** — 1330' PINE GULCH ROAD
> **CAMPING** — CHAW'SE INDIAN GRINDING ROCKS STATE PARK

AS YOU MIGHT GUESS, BECAUSE THERE IS ONLY ONE OUTLET FROM THIS DEEP VALLEY, AND THAT ROUTE IS THROUGH A NARROW GORGE, THE U.S. ARMY CORPS OF ENGINEERS AND UTILITY COMPANY HYDROELECTRIC POWER PLANNERS ARE SALIVATING OVER SUTTER CREEK CANYON. FOR THIS REASON VISIT VOLCANO FIRST — BEFORE DOING ANY OTHER RIDE IN THIS BOOK.

THE VILLAGE OF VOLCANO HAS AN OLD FASHIONED GENERAL STORE, A COUPLE OF QUAINT CAFES AND A GIFT SHOP. IF YOU CAN AFFORD AN INDOOR STAY THERE'S THE 120 YEAR OLD ST. GEORGE HOTEL ON THE SOUTH END OF MAIN ST.

IF YOU PREFER CAMPING MAKE RESERVATIONS AT CHAW'SE INDIAN GRINDING ROCK STATE HISTORIC PARK.

HALE SASH AND DOOR FACTORY — VOLCANO

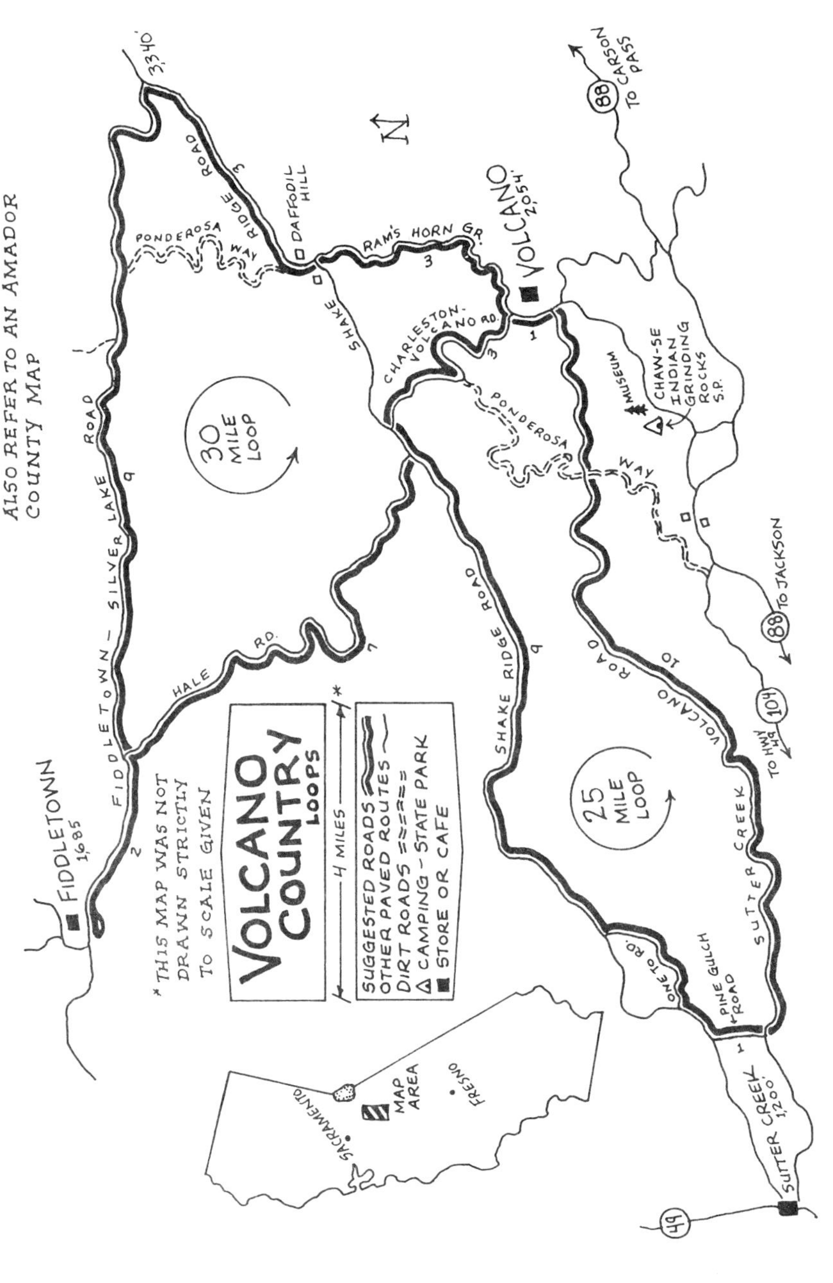

ALSO REFER TO AN AMADOR
COUNTY MAP

VOLCANO
COUNTRY
LOOPS

"THIS MAP WAS NOT
DRAWN STRICTLY
TO SCALE GIVEN

├──── 4 MILES ────┤
*

SUGGESTED ROADS ━━━
OTHER PAVED ROUTES ━━━
DIRT ROADS ======
△ CAMPING - STATE PARK
■ STORE OR CAFE

N ↑

FIDDLETOWN
1,685

FIDDLETOWN - SILVER LAKE ROAD

HALE R.D.

PONDEROSA WAY

RIDGE ROAD

3,340'

DAFFODIL HILL

SHAKE

RAM'S HORN GR.

30 MILE LOOP

CHARLESTON - VOLCANO RD.

PONDEROSA WAY

VOLCANO
2,054'

MUSEUM

CHAW-SE
INDIAN
GRINDING
ROCKS
S.P.

88 TO CARSON
TO PASS

88 TO JACKSON

104

TO HWY 49

VOLCANO ROAD

SHAKE RIDGE ROAD

25 MILE LOOP

SUTTER CREEK

PINE GULCH ROAD

ONE LO RD

SUTTER CREEK
1,200

49

SACRAMENTO

MAP AREA

FRESNO

61

23

YUBA CHALLENGE

WE NORMALLY START THIS RIDE IN THE SMALL VILLAGE OF CHALLENGE. DAY PARKING IS AVAILABLE AT THE U.S. FOREST SERVICE HEADQUARTERS. CHALLENGE SITS AT THE HIGH POINT OF THE LOWER (38 mi.) LOOP – SO, NORMALLY, IF YOU SEE NO SNOW IN CHALLENGE THE ROUTE WILL BE CLEAR THROUGHOUT THE REST OF THE LOOP (THERE ARE, HOWEVER, SOME NORTH-FACING STRETCHES ON OREGON HILL ROAD THAT HOLD ICE AND SNOW LONGER THAN ROADS AT HIGHER ELEVATIONS).

IF YOU'RE WEARING FAT TIRES YOU MIGHT PULL-OFF THE UPPER (15 mi.) LOOP AS A WARM-UP. WHEN YOU FIND THIS LOOP FREE OF ICE AND SNOW YOU CAN BE SURE THE LOWER LOOP IS FREE.

THIS IS ANOTHER OF THE "GREAT BANANA BELT RIDES" THAT ARE SO PLEASANT DURING THE SO-CALLED "OFF-SEASONS". CLEAR AND WARM IN AUTUMN WHEN THE VALLEY FLOOR IS SOCKED-IN WITH AGRI-SMOG, PERFECT IN WINTER WHEN THE LOWER FLATLANDS ARE SHIVERING UNDER A PERSISTANT TULE FOG AND SENSATIONAL IN SPRING WHEN WILDFLOWERS ABOUND. THE BEST LUNCH ON THE ROUTE DURING ANY SEASON IS AT THE CHALLENGE STORE. THE DELI THERE PUTS TOGETHER SOME GREAT SANDWICHES AND KEEPS THE WOODSTOVE ROARING.

THE COUNTRY STORE IN DOBBINS IS ALSO AN EXPERIENCE YOU OUGHT NOT MISS — A GOOD PLACE TO SNACK BEFORE RETURNING UPHILL TO CHALLENGE.

DISTANCES — 38 MILES AND 15 MILES

DIRECTION — COUNTERCLOCKWISE

HIGH POINT – UPPER LOOP 3,266' – MOUNT HOPE
LOWER LOOP 2,565' – CHALLENGE

LOW POINT – UPPER LOOP 2,501' – CHALLENGE
LOWER LOOP 1,530' – OREGON HOUSE

CAMPING – BURNT BRIDGE

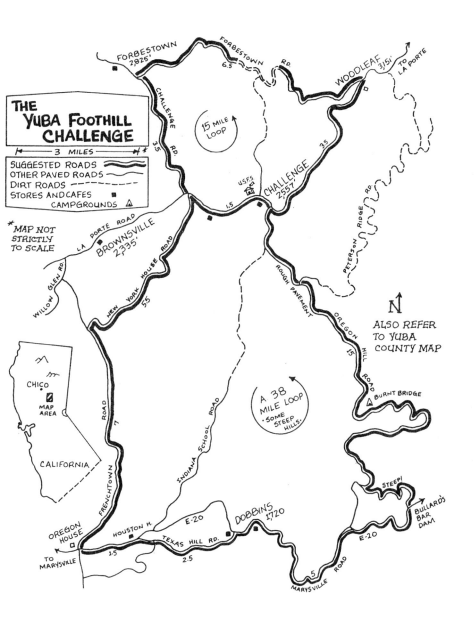

THE
YUBA FOOTHILL
CHALLENGE

|← 3 MILES →|*

SUGGESTED ROADS
OTHER PAVED ROADS
DIRT ROADS
STORES AND CAFES ■
CAMPGROUNDS ⛺

* MAP NOT
STRICTLY
TO SCALE

FORBESTOWN
2,825'

FORBESTOWN RD.
6.5

WOODLEAF 3,151'
TO LA PORTE

CHALLENGE RD.
3.5

15 MILE
LOOP

CHALLENGE 3.5

CHALLENGE
2,557'

U.S.F.S.

PETERSON RIDGE RD.

LA PORTE ROAD

BROWNSVILLE
2,335'

1.5

WILLOW GLEN RD.

NEW YORK HOUSE ROAD
5.5

ROUGH PAVEMENT

OREGON HILL ROAD
15

BURNT BRIDGE

N
ALSO REFER
TO YUBA
COUNTY MAP

CHICO
MAP
AREA

CALIFORNIA

FRENCHTOWN ROAD
7

INDIANA SCHOOL ROAD

A 38
MILE LOOP
· SOME
STEEP
HILLS ·

STEEP!

BULLARD'S
BAR
DAM

OREGON
HOUSE

TO
MARYSVILLE

HOUSTON H.
1.5

E-20
TEXAS HILL RD.
2.5

DOBBINS
1,720

E-20

5
MARYSVILLE ROAD

63

24

BUTTE COUNTY

TABLE MOUNTAIN

ONE OF THE PRIMO SHORT RIDES IN NORTHERN CALIFORNIA'S SIERRA FOOTHILLS. WILDFLOWERS ARE THE BIG REASON THIS RIDE RATES SO HIGH. LATE MARCH AND EARLY APRIL ARE "WILDFLOWER PRIMETIME" MONTHS — AVOID WILDFLOWER PRIMETIME WEEKENDS (ALSO POPULAR WITH MOTORISTS).

DISTANCE — 26 MILES

DIRECTION — CLOCKWISE

HIGH POINT — 1,315' CHEROKEE

LOW POINT — 170' OROVILLE

WIND — REVERSE DIRECTION OF RIDE WHEN WINDS ARE RAGING FROM NORTH.

OUR WEEKLY RIDES OVER TABLE MOUNTAIN THROUGHOUT THE SEVENTIES INSPIRED THE DEVELOPMENT OF THE CHICO VELO WILDFLOWER CENTURY, WHICH FAST BECAME THE BEST ATTENDED CENTURY RIDE IN RURAL NORTHERN CALIFORNIA.

I'M OFTEN TEMPTED TO TELL YOU WHERE TO
PARK THE CAR, WHAT TO BUY FOR LUNCH, AND HOW TO
FIND THE CLEANEST RESTROOMS, BUT I BELIEVE SOME
THINGS SHOULD BE LEFT UP TO THE JUDGEMENT OF THE
INDIVIDUAL. THE ONLY SERVICES AVAILABLE ON THIS LOOP
ARE IN THE CITY OF OROVILLE, ONLY A COUPLE OF BLOCKS
FROM THE SOUTHERNMOST POINT OF THE RIDE.

THE TABLE MOUNTAIN CIRCUIT CAN BE AN
OUTSTANDING JAUNT ANYTIME OF THE YEAR,
AS SNOW IS A RARITY AT 1,300' IN THIS
REGION OF NORTHERN
CALIFORNIA.

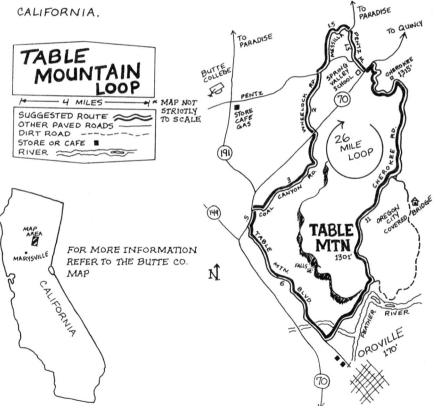

FOR MORE INFORMATION
REFER TO THE BUTTE CO.
MAP

25
TEHAMA AND SHASTA COUNTIES
YANA FOOTHILLS

...OUR FAVORITE WINTER TRAINING GROUNDS. THE PAYNE'S, BATTLE AND ASH CREEK DRAINAGES HAVE A LITTLE OF EVERYTHING TO OFFER, YET, THESE ROADS ARE SELDOM TRAVELLED BY MOTOR CARS. THE BUSIEST STRETCH WILL BE THE 6.5 MILE DOWNHILL BELOW SHINGLETOWN ON HWY 44.

A FEW WORDS SHOULD BE PUT FORTH ABOUT WILSON HILL ROAD NORTH OF MANTON... STEEP, STEEP AND STEEPER!
BEST PLACE TO START THE RIDE — THE SAFETY HARBOR CAFE IN PAYNE'S CREEK. THEY ALSO HAVE THE BEST FOOD.

ALSO REFER TO SHASTA AND TEHAMA COUNTY MAPS

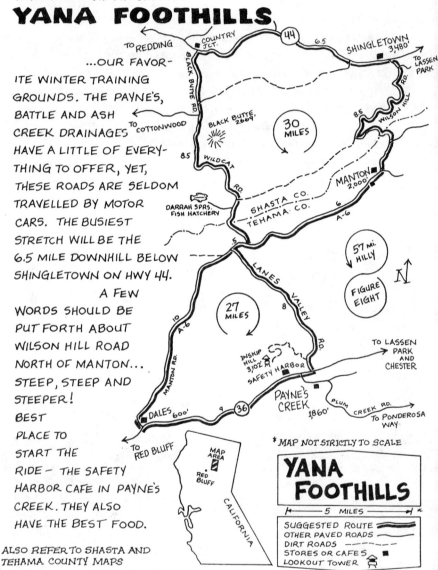

TO REDDING
COUNTRY JCT.
44 6.5 SHINGLETOWN 3,480'
BLACK BUTTE RD.
TO LASSEN PARK
BLACK BUTTE 2669'
30 MILES
8.5 WILSON HILL RD.
TO COTTONWOOD
8.5 WILDCAT RD.
MANTON 2,000'
DARRAH SPRS. FISH HATCHERY
SHASTA CO.
TEHAMA CO.
6 A-6
5
57 mi. HILLY
LANES VALLEY
FIGURE EIGHT
N
27 MILES
8
10 A-6
RD.
TO LASSEN PARK AND CHESTER
INSKIP HILL 3,102'
SAFETY HARBOR
MANTON RD.
PAYNE'S CREEK 1,860'
PLUM CREEK RD.
TO PONDEROSA WAY
9 36
DALES 600'
TO RED BLUFF

MAP AREA
RED BLUFF
CALIFORNIA

* MAP NOT STRICTLY TO SCALE
YANA FOOTHILLS
|← 5 MILES →|
SUGGESTED ROUTE
OTHER PAVED ROADS
DIRT ROADS
STORES OR CAFES
LOOKOUT TOWER

26
SHASTA COUNTY
KIP'S METRIC CENTURY

LIVING THE SIMPLE LIFE, THE BICYCLE HIS ONLY MACHINE, HE LIVED IN A CABIN ON PHILLIPS ROAD — WITHOUT PLUMBING OR ELECTRICITY OR TELEVISION OR T.V. DINNERS. AN AXE, A LANTERN AND A BICYCLE... AND FOLKS THOUGHT HE WAS CRAZY?

DISTANCE — 60 MILES
DIRECTION — CLOCKWISE
STARTING POINT— PALO CEDRO - WE USUALLY PARK AT THE COMMUNITY CHURCH.
HIGH POINT- 2,990' ON PHILLIPS ROAD
LOW POINT — 461' IN PALO CEDRO - CAMPING ON SHASTA LK. AT JONES VALLEY

HIS SPIRIT ROAMS THESE HILLS — SOARING DOWN BUZZARD ROOST, BULLSKIN AND FERN ROADS - ON A BIKE SOME FIFTY YEARS BEFORE MANY OF US SHIFTED OUR FIRST GEAR. KIP PHILLIPS SCOUTED THESE HILLS LONG BEFORE THEY WERE FENCED, GRAZED AND INVADED BY PAVEMENT.

HE GAVE LOG-TRUCKS FITS — SLOW TO YIELD, BROUGHT THEM TO A HALT BY HOLDING TIGHT TO HIS SADDLE AND HIS RIGHTFUL PLACE ON THE THOROUGHFARE.

HE RODE INTO THE WILDERNESS AND "DOWN BELOW", TO THE VILLAGES ON THE VALLEY FLOOR, CONFUSIN' FOLKS WITH HIS "SIMPLE LIFE" RAMBLINGS. CLOVER MOUN-TAIN, SILVER LAKE AND OAK RUN...KIP PHILLIPS TOLD FAN-TASTIC STORIES, FISH STORIES FROM A MIND UNBRIDLED BY TIMEX, ROLEX AND THE NBC NIGHTLY NEWS.

THESE HILLS ARE ALSO THE PREFERRED TRAINING ROUTES FOR THE SHASTA WHEELMEN AND REDDING VELO - AND FOR GOOD REASONS — THEY ARE LIGHTLY TRAVELLED ROADS WITH GREAT VIEWS OF MT. SHASTA, LASSEN PEAK, THE TRINITY ALPS AND THE UPPER END OF THE SACRAMENTO VALLEY.

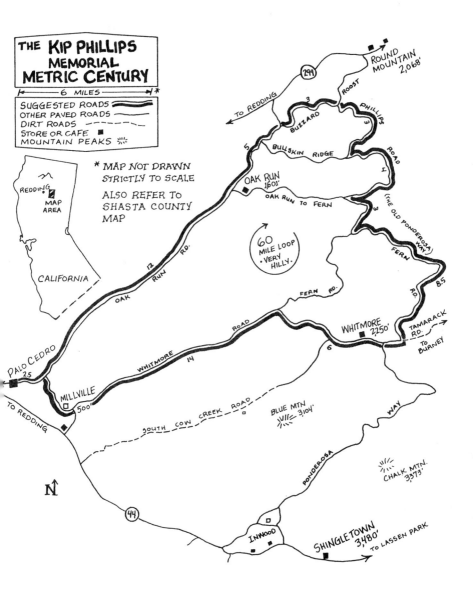

THE **KIP PHILLIPS**
MEMORIAL
METRIC CENTURY

6 MILES ⟶ *

SUGGESTED ROADS ▬▬▬
OTHER PAVED ROADS ▬
DIRT ROADS ----
STORE OR CAFE ■
MOUNTAIN PEAKS ☼

* MAP NOT DRAWN
STRICTLY TO SCALE

ALSO REFER TO
SHASTA COUNTY
MAP

REDDING
MAP
AREA

CALIFORNIA

ROUND
MOUNTAIN
2,068'

299

TO REDDING

ROOST

3

BUZZARD

PHILLIPS

5

BULLSKIN RIDGE

3

ROAD

OAK RUN
1,601'

OAK RUN TO FERN

4

(THE OLD PONDEROSA) WAY

3

60
MILE LOOP
• VERY
HILLY.

FERN

12

OAK RUN RD.

FERN RD.

ROAD

8.5

FERN RD.

WHITMORE
2,750'

TAMARACK
RD.

PALO CEDRO
2.5

WHITMORE

14

6

TO
BURNEY

TO REDDING

MILLVILLE
500'

SOUTH COW CREEK ROAD

BLUE MTN.
3,104'

WAY

PONDEROSA

CHALK MTN.
3,373'

N

44

INWOOD

SHINGLETOWN
3,480'

TO LASSEN PARK

69

27

TRINITY COUNTY

WILDWOOD-PEANUT LOOP

HAYFORK IS A STRUGGLING LUMBER TOWN ON STATE HIGHWAY 3 SOME THIRTY MILES SOUTH OF WEAVERVILLE AND THE TRINITY RIVER. THE AMAZING THING, TO ME, ABOUT HAYFORK IS THE FIFTEEN YEAR SURVIVAL OF SALLY'S GOLD COUNTRY NATURAL FOODS STORE.

STARTING POINT – HAYFORK
DISTANCE – 45 MILES
DIRECTION – COUNTERCLOCKWISE
HIGH POINT – 4,225' ON HWY 36
LOW POINT 2,323' HAYFORK

THIS IS AN INDICATION THAT THE HILLS ABOVE HAYFORK ARE ALIVE WITH COUNTERCULTURE TYPES, HEALTH NUTS AND EVEN A FEW AVID CYCLISTS.

ONE SUCH HAYFORK AREA BIKEE INVITED ME TO VISIT SEVERAL YEARS AGO TO EXPERIENCE "A NEAR-PERFECT CENTURY RIDE." IT STARTED WITH AN OUT AND BACK SPIN TO HYAMPOM (46 MILES), THIS QUIET WINDING ROAD ALONG HAYFORK CREEK TO WHERE IT EMPTIES INTO THE SOUTH FORK OF THE TRINITY. I CAREFULLY EXPLAINED TO MY HAYFORK INFORMANT THAT AN OUT AND BACK JAUNT TO START OFF A CENTURY RIDE MIGHT NOT GET GREAT REVIEWS AMONGST URBAN BIKE CLUB CENTURY CRITICS, (HE WANTED TO PROMOTE THIS RIDE AS AN ANNUAL EVENT) ... "YOU WAIT," HE COUNTERED, "THE LAST HALF IS A LOOP LIKE NO OTHER — THE WILDWOOD-PEANUT LOOP MAY BE THE BEST IN THE STATE!"

HE WAS RIGHT, WITH THE EXCEPTION OF THE FINAL THREE SEMI-BUSY MILES ALONG STATE HWY 3 INTO HAYFORK, THIS IS ONE CLASSIC LOOP.

IF YOU ARE RIDING ON FAT TIRES YOU MIGHT TRY THIRTEEN DIPS RD. – A ROLLER COASTER "SHORTCUT."

70

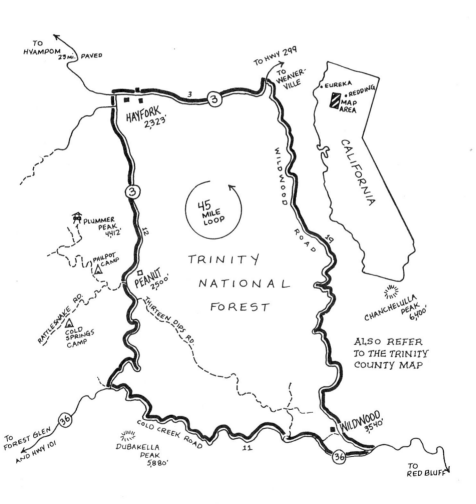

71

28
COLUSA COUNTY
OUT OF SITES

MY GOOD FRIEND FRAN FARLEY (REKNOWN CLASSICAL MUSIC HOST) AND I TOURED THE SITES GENERAL STORE (NOW CLOSED) DURING A RESTBREAK ON A CENTURY RIDE BACK IN THE EARLY EIGHTIES. THERE·IN WE FOUND A LARGE COILED COPPERHEAD FROM MISSOURI, A SET OF JAME'S WHISTLER'S MOTHER'S KNITTING NEEDLES FROM NEW ENGLAND AND A TRANSPLANTED 1929 PHONE BOOTH FROM DOWNTOWN CHICAGO, ILLINOIS. SITES, POP. 11, HAD MUCH TO OFFER THE ATTENTIVE TOURIST.

AS WE ROLLED OUT OF TOWN I ASKED FRAN IF HE'D EVER SEEN A COPPERHEAD BEFORE,

"NO! WASN'T THAT OUT OF SITES!" HE GUFFAWED.

ACTUALLY, THIS LOOP IS "OUT OF SITES" IF YOU LIKE QUIET COUNTRY LANES THROUGH DRAMATIC TOPOGRAPHY. RIDE IT IN THE SPRING OR EVEN LATE WINTER AND YOU'LL WONDER IF YOU'VE BEEN "BEAMED" TO IRELAND OR NEW ZEALAND — SHEEP SPRINKLED OVER VERDANT HILLSIDES ACCENTED BY VIBRANT DISPLAYS OF COAST RANGE WILDFLOWERS.

LODOGA HAS A SMALL STORE WITH A VERY LIMITED INVENTORY OF FOODSTUFFS (A GOOD SUPPLY OF V8 JUICE, HOWEVER). IT MIGHT BE BEST TO PACK YOUR OWN LUNCH ON THIS LOOP. WATER IS AVAILABLE IN LEESVILLE, LODOGA AND SITES.

STARTING POINT- MAXWELL

DISTANCE — 62 MILES

DIRECTION — CLOCKWISE

HIGH POINT — 1845' GRAPEVINE PASS

LOW POINT — 80' MAXWELL

LODGING — 'WILBUR' A CLOTHING OPTIONAL HOT SPRING TWELVE MI. SO. OF LEESVILLE

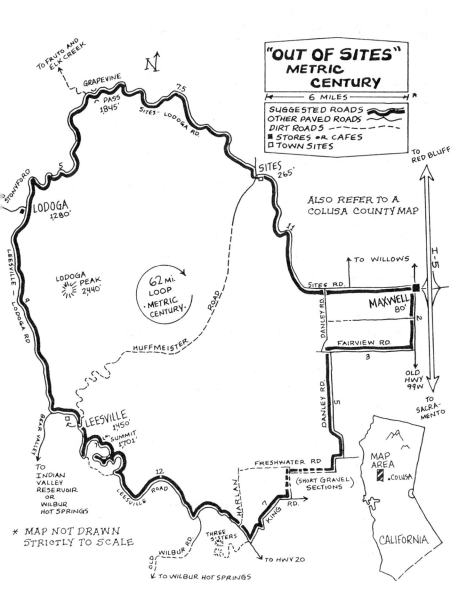

"OUT OF SITES"
METRIC
CENTURY

├── 6 MILES ──┤ *
SUGGESTED ROADS
OTHER PAVED ROADS
DIRT ROADS
■ STORES or CAFES
□ TOWN SITES

TO FRUTO AND
ELK CREEK
GRAPEVINE
N
7.5
PASS
1845'
SITES - LODOGA RD.

STONYFORD
5
SITES
265'

LODOGA
1280'

ALSO REFER TO A
COLUSA COUNTY MAP

TO RED BLUFF

TO WILLOWS

LODOGA PEAK
2440'

62 MI.
LOOP
METRIC
CENTURY

ROAD

SITES RD.

DANLEY RD.

MAXWELL
80'

I-5

HUFFMEISTER

FAIRVIEW RD.
3

LEESVILLE - LODOGA RD.
9

OLD HWY 99W

TO SACRA-
MENTO

BEAR VALLEY

LEESVILLE
1450'
SUMMIT
1701'

DANLEY RD.
5

MAP AREA
COLUSA

TO INDIAN
VALLEY
RESERVOIR
OR
WILBUR
HOT SPRINGS

LEESVILLE ROAD
12

FRESHWATER RD.

(SHORT GRAVEL)
SECTIONS

* MAP NOT DRAWN
STRICTLY TO SCALE

HARLAN
7

KING RD.

CALIFORNIA

THREE SISTERS

WILBUR RD.

TO HWY 20

OLD

TO WILBUR HOT SPRINGS

73

29

LAKE AND NAPA COUNTIES

POPE VALLEY · KNOXVILLE

I WAS FIRST INTRO-
DUCED TO THE WESTERN AND
NORTHERN PORTIONS OF THIS LOOP
WHILE RIDING THE DAVIS DOUBLE
CENTURY. I WAS SURPRISED AT
HOW QUIET THE ROADS BETWEEN
POPE VALLEY AND LOWER LAKE
WERE DURING A LATE SPRING
WEEKEND, AND YET SO NEAR THE
BUSY NAPA VALLEY AND CLEAR LAKE REGIONS.

STARTING POINT —
   MIDDLETOWN 1,110'
DISTANCE — 82 MILES
DIRECTION —
   COUNTERCLOCKWISE
HIGH POINT — 2470'
   NEAR REIFF
LOW POINT — 440' AT
   LAKE BERRYESSA

THE EASTERN HALF OF THIS LOOP IS EXCEPTION-
ALLY TRANQUIL ON WEEKENDS.

IF YOU ARE RIDING IN A COUNTERCLOCKWISE
DIRECTION CARRY PLENTY OF WATER FROM PUTAH CREEK
PARK (ON LAKE BERRYESSA) TO LOWER LAKE (35 MILES).
WE FOUND A PAINTED TURTLE ALONG THIS STRETCH NEAR
THE TOWNSITE OF KNOXVILLE. IT WAS A SIMMERING HOT
SUMMER DAY, THE HILLS WERE BROWN AND THIRSTY AND
MR. TURTLE WAS ATTEMPTING TO CROSS A SHADY STRETCH
OF PATCHWORK PAVEMENT — POSSIBLY IN ROUTE TO THE
REMAINING TRICKLE IN ETICUERA CREEK. HE SAT IN THE
MIDDLE OF THE ROAD WITH LEGS, ARMS AND HEAD TUCKED
AWAY... WAITING FOR NIGHTFALL, AND COOLER TRAVEL?

WE PICKED HIM UP AND CARRIED HIM 100 YDS.
DOWN A ROCKY SLOPE AND SET HIM NEXT TO THE CREEK.
HIS HEAD POKED OUT — WE LAUGHED AND HE IMMEDIATE-
LY DOVE INTO THE CREEK, THANKFUL, I'M SURE, FOR THE
DAY'S WORTH OF CALORIES WE SAVED HIM IN HIS TRAVELS.

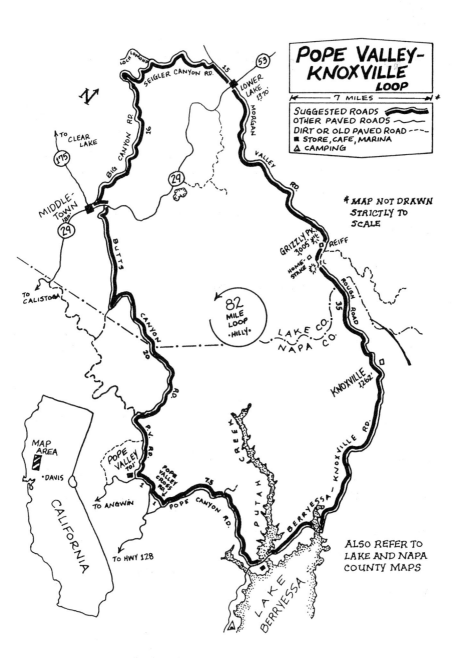

POPE VALLEY-
KNOXVILLE
LOOP

7 MILES

SUGGESTED ROADS
OTHER PAVED ROADS
DIRT OR OLD PAVED ROAD ----
■ STORE, CAFE, MARINA
△ CAMPING

* MAP NOT DRAWN
STRICTLY TO
SCALE

N

TO CLEAR LAKE
175

LOCK LOMOND
SEIGLER CANYON RD.
15
53
LOWER LAKE 1370'
MORGAN
VALLEY
RD.
BIG CANYON RD.
16
29
MIDDLE-TOWN 1120'
29
BUTTS
CANYON
RD.
20
TO CALISTOGA

82
MILE
LOOP
•HILLY•

GRIZZLY PK. 3005'
HOME-STAKE
REIFF
ROUGH ROAD
35
LAKE CO.
NAPA CO.
KNOXVILLE 1262'
BERRYESSA-KNOXVILLE RD.

MAP AREA
•DAVIS

CALIFORNIA

P.V. RD.
POPE VALLEY 701'
POPE VALLEY CROSS RD.
1
TO ANGWIN
1
POPE CANYON RD.
7.5
PUTAH CREEK
BERRYESSA.

TO HWY 128

△
LAKE BERRYESSA.

ALSO REFER TO
LAKE AND NAPA
COUNTY MAPS

75

30

ALAMEDA, SAN JOAQUIN, STANISLAUS AND SANTA CLARA CO.

JACK'S LEMONADE LOOP

NOW CALLED, "JACK'S ONLY SLIGHTLY RADIOACTIVE LEMONADE LOOP." GOVERNMENT RESEARCHERS RECENTLY REVEALED THAT THE WINES OF THE LIVERMORE VALLEY ARE "ONLY SLIGHTLY TAINTED BY RADIOACTIVITY." THEY ARE, HOWEVER, "THE MOST RADIOACTIVE WINES PRODUCED IN THE STATE OF CALIFORNIA."

JACK WALDORF IS A RIDING BUDDY OF MINE WHO LIVES NEAR MODESTO. HE'S BEEN RIDING THIS LOOP FOR YEARS, "BUT NEVER AT A BLISTERING PACE, MIND YOU, YET, OFTEN DURING TIMES OF BLISTERING VALLEY HEAT."

WE WERE CLIMBING THROUGH A FROZEN CALIFORNIA CASCADE RANGE FOREST WHEN JACK TOLD ME HIS LEMONADE STORY, "THERE'S A LITTLE COWBOY BAR OUT THERE IN THE SAN ANTONIO VALLEY — IT'S AT THE BASE OF THE CLIMB UP THE EAST SIDE OF MT. HAMILTON. I HAD ALREADY CONSUMED ALL OF MY WATER AND IT WAS A LONG WAY... DID I SAY IT WAS HOT? YEA, IT WAS HOT AND THE AIR WAS AS DRY AS A POPCORN FART... LONG WAY TO LIVERMORE. THE WATER QUALITY OUT THERE'S A BIT QUESTIONABLE BUT I SEE THIS SIGN OFFERING 'LEMONADE BY THE PITCHER'. WE PULL IN AND 'FORE YA KNOW IT I'VE FINISHED MY PITCHER. THE BARKEEP LOOKS BACK OVER HIS SHOULDER AS HE WASHES A GLASS IN THE SINK, "HEY, I WAS GONNA GET YOU A GLASS." I LOOK UP AND SAY, "THAT WOULD BE GREAT, AND HOW ABOUT ANOTHER PITCHER OF LEMONADE?"

STARTING POINT —
LIVERMORE
DISTANCE — 91 MILES
DIRECTION —
CLOCKWISE
HIGH POINT —
2,951' S.A.V. ROAD
LOW POINT —
158' AQUEDUCT
WEATHER — SUMMER-HOT,
WINTER - MILD

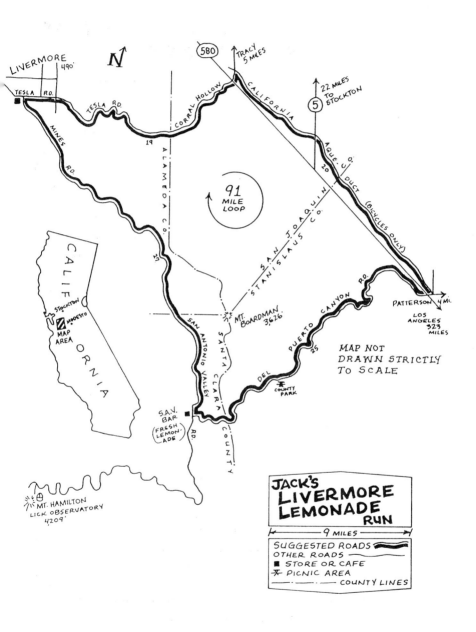

N

LIVERMORE 490'

TESLA RD.

TESLA RD.

MINES RD.

CORRAL HOLLOW

ALAMEDA CO.

19

580

TRACY 5 MILES

CALIFORNIA

22 MILES TO STOCKTON

5

AQUE-DUCT (BICYCLES ONLY)

20

SAN JOAQUIN

STANISLAUS CO.

91 MILE LOOP

25

MT. BOARDMAN 3626

PUERTO CANYON RD.

25

PATTERSON 4 MI.

LOS ANGELES 323 MILES

SAN ANTONIO VALLEY

SANTA CLARA COUNTY

DEL

COUNTY PARK

MAP NOT DRAWN STRICTLY TO SCALE

CALIFORNIA

Stockton
Modesto
MAP AREA

S.A.V. BAR (FRESH LEMON-ADE)

RD.

MT. HAMILTON LICK OBSERVATORY 4209'

JACK'S
LIVERMORE
LEMONADE
RUN

9 MILES

SUGGESTED ROADS
OTHER ROADS
■ STORE OR CAFE
✕ PICNIC AREA
COUNTY LINES

77

HIGH COUNTRY RIDES

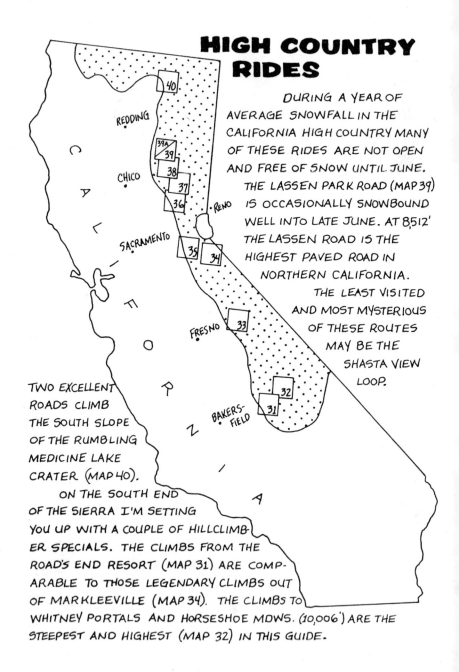

DURING A YEAR OF AVERAGE SNOWFALL IN THE CALIFORNIA HIGH COUNTRY MANY OF THESE RIDES ARE NOT OPEN AND FREE OF SNOW UNTIL JUNE. THE LASSEN PARK ROAD (MAP 39) IS OCCASIONALLY SNOWBOUND WELL INTO LATE JUNE. AT 8,512' THE LASSEN ROAD IS THE HIGHEST PAVED ROAD IN NORTHERN CALIFORNIA.

THE LEAST VISITED AND MOST MYSTERIOUS OF THESE ROUTES MAY BE THE SHASTA VIEW LOOP.

TWO EXCELLENT ROADS CLIMB THE SOUTH SLOPE OF THE RUMBLING MEDICINE LAKE CRATER (MAP 40).

ON THE SOUTH END OF THE SIERRA I'M SETTING YOU UP WITH A COUPLE OF HILLCLIMBER SPECIALS. THE CLIMBS FROM THE ROAD'S END RESORT (MAP 31) ARE COMPARABLE TO THOSE LEGENDARY CLIMBS OUT OF MARKLEEVILLE (MAP 34). THE CLIMBS TO WHITNEY PORTALS AND HORSESHOE MDWS. (10,006') ARE THE STEEPEST AND HIGHEST (MAP 32) IN THIS GUIDE.

31
ROAD'S END BASECAMP

A HILL CLIMBER'S HIGH COUNTRY DREAM — THE SOUTHERN SIERRA VERSION OF THE MARKLEEVILLE BASECAMP (RIDE NO. 34).

CABINS ARE FOR RENT AND THE COFFEE IS BREWING IN THE SMALL KERN RIVER "GAS STOP" KNOWN AS ROAD'S END, OPEN FROM MAY THROUGH NOVEMBER. DURING MOST OF THIS SIX MONTH PERIOD YOU'LL FIND THE RIDING UNSURPASSED BY ANY OTHER ROADS IN THE WEST — DRAMATIC CLIMBS BENEATH GRANITE SPIRES AND DOMES (THE 60 MILE ROUNDTRIPPER UP THE KERN RIVER CANYON THAT RUNS BELOW THE NEEDLES AND UP TO A POINT BELOW CASTLE ROCK), ANOTHER 60+ MILE RIDE TO PARKER PASS AND PONDEROSA THAT ROLLS BELOW A GROVE OF STATELY 3500+ YEAR OLD SEQUOIA GIGANTEUM AND COULD INCLUDE A RUSTIC CAFE STOP AT 7,200' IN PONDEROSA, AND THE GRAND DADDY CLIMB OF 5,600' VERTICAL TO SHERMAN PASS AND AN ADDITIONAL 4,000' OF CLIMBING BEFORE REACHING BLACKROCK MTN. AND THE SOUTHERN EDGE OF THE GOLDEN TROUT WILDERNESS. 210 MILES OF QUIET PAVEMENT IN WILD AND UNDEVELOPED SOUTHERN TULARE COUNTY.

A WEEKEND HERE MIGHT FUEL PLEASANT IN-THE-SADDLE DREAMS THAT STICK WITH YOU FOR DECADES. I FIRST EXPLORED THESE ROADS IN THE EARLY SEVENTIES, WHEN JOHNSONDALE HAD AN OPERATING LUMBER MILL AND A GENERAL STORE AND SHERMAN PASS WAS AN UNPAVED LOGGING ROAD.

STARTING POINT—	ROAD'S END, MT. 99
DISTANCE — 210 MILES TOTAL	
DIRECTION — OUT AND BACK	
HIGHEST POINT — 9,200' SHERMAN PASS	
LOWEST POINT — 3,600' ROAD'S END, MT. 99	

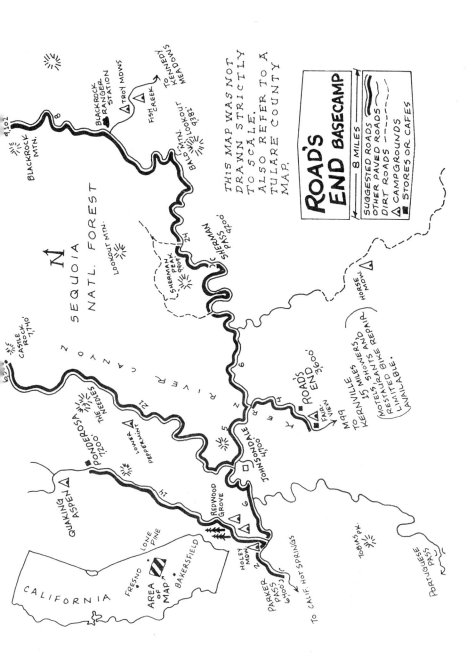

ROAD'S END BASECAMP

8 MILES

Suggested Roads
Other Paved Roads
Dirt Roads
△ Campgrounds
■ Stores or Cafes

THIS MAP WAS NOT DRAWN STRICTLY TO SCALE. ALSO REFER TO A TULARE COUNTY MAP.

SEQUOIA NATL. FOREST

BLACKROCK MTN. 9,102'

BLACKROCK RANGER STATION
△ TROY MDWS
△ FISH CREEK
TO KENNEDY MEADOWS

8

BALD MTN. LOOKOUT 9,382'

LOOKOUT MTN.

SHERMAN PEAK 9,909'

SHERMAN PASS 9,200'

24

CASTLE ROCK 7,710'

KERN RIVER CANYON

THE NEEDLES 8,200'

PONDEROSA 7,200'

△ LOWER PEPPERMINT

12

QUAKING ASPEN △

14

△ REDWOOD GROVE

6

JOHNSONDALE 4,700'

5

N

3

HORSE MDW △

6

△ ROAD'S END 3,600'

■ FAIR-VIEW

4

M99

TO KERNVILLE 15 MILES
(MOTELS, SHOWERS, RESTAURANTS, BIKE REPAIR LIMITED AVAILABLE.)

SEQUOIA NATL. FOREST

N

CALIFORNIA

FRESNO
LONE PINE
AREA OF MAP
BAKERSFIELD

PARKER PASS 6,400'

△ HOLEY MDW

2

To CALIF. HOT SPRINGS

TOBIAS PK.

PORTUGUESE PASS

81

32
INYO COUNTY
LONE PINE HORSESHOE

THERE'S MAGIC IN THE AIR ON THE DRY SIDE OF THE SIERRA NEVADA RANGE. WAVES OF HIGH CIRRUS CLOUDS BACKED BY A BATTALION OF CUMULONIMBUS FORMATIONS ARE OFTEN SEEN LEANING EASTWARD FROM THE CREST OF 14,000 FT. PEAKS OVER THE 4,000 FT. OWENS VALLEY.

STARTING POINT — LONE PINE
DISTANCE — 63 MILES TO COMPLETE ENTIRE HORSESHOE
DIRECTION — RIDER'S CHOICE
HIGH POINT — 10,006' AT HORSESHOE MDW.
LOW POINT — 3,730' LONE PINE

THE ALABAMA HILLS (JUST WEST OF LONE PINE) AND THE OWENS VALLEY ARE MOST OFTEN OPEN TO RIDING YEAR-AROUND. THE HOGBACK, MOVIE FLAT EIGHTEEN MILE FAT TIRE LOOP IS USUALLY OPEN BUT BEWARE OF FLASH FLOOD DANGER DURING STORMS.

THE CLIMBS TO WHITNEY PORTALS (8,006') AND HORSESHOE MEADOWS (10,006') ARE LIMITED AT LEAST SIX MONTHS A YEAR BY SNOW AND ICE ACCUMULATIONS ON THE ROADWAYS. WE'VE FOUND BOTH OF THESE CLIMBS TO BE OPEN FOR CYCLING BETWEEN JULY 4 AND THANKSGIVING HOLIDAYS DURING MOST YEARS. HAZARDOUS SAND AND GRAVEL PATCHES ARE ALWAYS A PROBLEM ON BOTH CLIMBS.

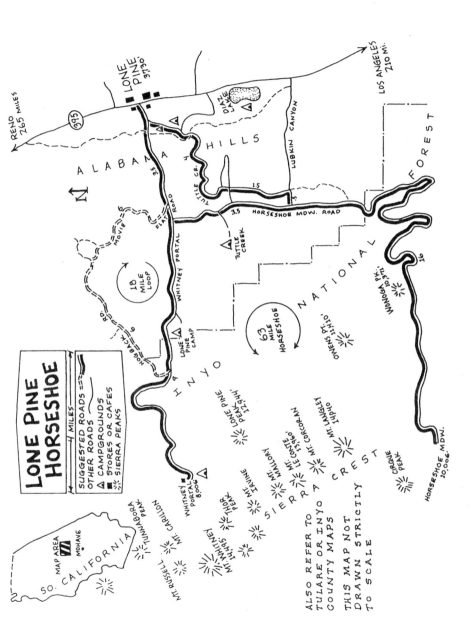

LONE PINE HORSESHOE

MILES

SUGGESTED ROADS
OTHER ROADS
CAMPGROUNDS
STORES OR CAFES
SIERRA PEAKS

LONE PINE 3,730'

RENO 265 MILES

395

LOS ANGELES 210 MI.

ALABAMA HILLS

DIAZ LAKE

LUBKIN CANYON

N

18 MILE LOOP

MOVIE

FLAT

TUTTLE CR. RD.

3.5

WHITNEY PORTAL ROAD

HORSESHOE MDW. ROAD

3.5

TUTTLE CREEK

16

NATIONAL FOREST

WONOGA PK. 10,371'

OWENS PT. 11,110'

HORSEBACK RD.

9

LONE PINE CAMP

INYO

63 MILE HORSESHOE

WHITNEY PORTAL 8,000'

LONE PINE PEAK 12,944'

MT. MALLORY

MT. IRVINE

MT. LE CONTE 13,960'

MT. CORCORAN

MT. LANGLEY 14,040

SIERRA CREST

CIRQUE PEAK

HORSESHOE MDW. 10,006.

SO. CALIFORNIA

MAP AREA

MOHAVE

TUNNABORA PEAK

MT. RUSSELL

MT. CARILLON

THOR PEAK

MT. WHITNEY 14,496'

MT. HITCHCOCK

ALSO REFER TO TULARE OR INYO COUNTY MAPS

THIS MAP NOT DRAWN STRICTLY TO SCALE

33
FRESNO COUNTY
HEADWATERS 88

"HAD JOHN MUIR OWNED A MULTI-SPEED BIKE
THIS WOULD HAVE BEEN HIS FAVORITE RIDE."
— SUZANNE MUIR

THE BEST APPROACH TO THIS RIDE IS TO PARK OR
CAMP NEAR THE EAST END OF HUNTINGTON LAKE. FROM HERE
YOU CAN EASILY BREAK THE 88 MILES OF PAVEMENT DEPICTED
HERE INTO TWO SINGLE DAY RIDES (RIDE THE DIRT TO MT. TOM ON
THE THIRD DAY).

ON THE FIRST DAY RIDE WESTWARD ALONG THE NORTH-
SHORE. JUST BEYOND THE END OF THE OF THE LAKE THE ROAD
MAKES A SPECTACULAR DROP TO BIG CREEK (A SO. CAL. EDISON
COMPANY TOWN AT THE BASE OF POLISHED GRANITE DOMES AND
SPIRES). IN THE "HEART" OF BIG CREEK YOU'LL PASS THE BIG
CREEK HOTEL WHERE ONE OF MY RIDING BUDDIES, ED HURLEY,
TELLS ME OF SLEEPING MORE THAN A
FEW DECADES AGO, "A GREAT
PLACE TO SPEND THE
NIGHT—OPEN RAFTERS;
QUITE RUSTIC. THE
BEDS HAD SQUEAKY
SPRINGS —IN FACT,
I REMEMBER ONE
NIGHT NEXT TO THE
NEWLYWED SUITE;
THIS HANDSOME
YOUNG COUPLE
KEPT THOSE
SPRINGS SQUEAK-
ING ALL NIGHT.
JUST AS I'D DOZE
OFF THEY'D BREAK

INTO GIGGLING; I DIDN'T GET MUCH SLEEP THAT NIGHT.

THE ROAD CLIMBS OUT OF THE BIG CREEK DRAINAGE AND OVER THE SHOULDER OF MUSICK MOUNTAIN BEFORE DROPPING GENTLY TO HIGHWAY 168. UNLESS YOU NEED THE SERVICES OF THE BUSINESS STRIP ALONG THE WESTSHORE OF SHAVER LAKE, HANG A LEFT ON HIGHWAY 168 AND COMMENCE CLIMBING ON A WIDE AND USUALLY QUIET TARMAC

DISTANCES— 33 MILE LOOP
  55 MILE OUT AND BACK TO LAKES
  88 MILES - ALL PAVED SECTIONS MAPPED

DIRECTION — 33 MILE LOOP, COUNTERCLOCKWISE

HIGH POINT - KAISER PASS 9,176'

LOW POINT — BIG CREEK 4,875'

CAMPGROUNDS — TOO NUMEROUS TO LIST. MANY SITES ON HUNTINGTON LAKE, EDISON AND FLORENCE LAKES

TO TAMARACK RIDGE SUMMIT 7,550'. OVER THE TOP, YOU IMMEDIATELY CATCH SIGHT OF HUNTINGTON LAKE AND BEGIN THE LONG DOWNHILL BACK TO CAMP.

THE SECOND DAY (OR SAMEDAY AFTERNOON IF YOU ARE FEELING SPUNKY) RIDE, TO FLORENCE AND EDISON LAKES, NORMALLY CAN'T BE ACCOMPLISHED EARLIER THAN MEMORIAL DAY WEEKEND. ONE YEAR IN LATE APRIL I FOUND THE KAISER PASS ROAD AS A NARROW FRESHLY PLOWED ONE-LANE TUNNEL THROUGH 10 FOOT SNOWBANKS – A BIT SLUSHY, BUT ON FAT TIRES A GREAT CROSSING (WATCH-OUT FOR THE PLOW MAKING ITS RETURN TRIP.). KAISER PASS IS AT 9,175'. ONCE ON THE BACKSIDE OF KAISER YOU ARE IN THE WILD AND REMOTE SOUTH FORK COUNTRY WHERE YOU'LL FIND MONO HOT SPRINGS, LAKE THOMAS A. EDISON, FLORENCE LAKE, THE ROAD INTO MT. TOM LOOKOUT (9,020'), AND SEVERAL TRAILHEADS INTO THE JOHN MUIR WILDERNESS.

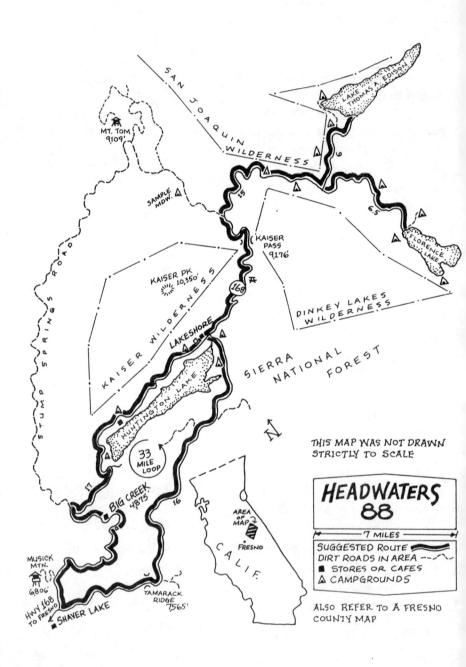

SAN JOAQUIN

WILDERNESS

LAKE THOMAS A. EDISON

MT. TOM
9109'

SAMPLE
MDW.

15

6

6.5

FLORENCE
LAKE

KAISER
PASS
9176

KAISER PK
10,350'

168

KAISER WILDERNESS

DINKEY LAKES
WILDERNESS

LAKESHORE

SIERRA   NATIONAL   FOREST

STUMP SPRINGS ROAD

HUNTINGTON LAKE

33
MILE
LOOP

N

THIS MAP WAS NOT DRAWN
STRICTLY TO SCALE

17

BIG CREEK
4,875'

16

AREA
OF
MAP

FRESNO

C A L I F.

**HEADWATERS
88**

7 MILES

SUGGESTED ROUTE
DIRT ROADS IN AREA ------
■ STORES OR CAFES
△ CAMPGROUNDS

MUSICK
MTN.

6806'

HWY 168
TO FRESNO

TAMARACK
RIDGE
7,565'

SHAVER LAKE

ALSO REFER TO A FRESNO
COUNTY MAP

34
ALPINE COUNTY
MARKLEEVILLE

TRUELY A MID-
SUMMER / AUTUMN BICYCLIST'S
NIRVANA. LOTS OF OPTIONS FOR
LODGING — STAY AT THE ALPINE
HOTEL IN DOWNTOWN MARKLEE-
VILLE, OR IF YOU'RE INTO NOISY
NIGHTLIFE AND PLUSH ACCOMOD-
ATIONS SOUTH LAKE TAHOE IS 32
MILES TO THE NORTH OR, SAY YOU
ARE THE OUTDOOR TYPE — YOU
CAN CAMP AT GROVER HOT SPRINGS

STARTING POINT—
   MARKLEEVILLE
DISTANCE— TOTAL ALL
   LEGS 157 MILES
DIRECTION— ALL OUT AND
   BACK ROUTES
HIGH POINTS—
   MONITOR PASS 8300'
   EBBETTS PASS 8,731'
   PACIFIC GRADE 8,050'
   DAGGETT PASS 7,334'
LOW POINT— CARSON
   VALLEY, NEV. 4,725'

STATE PARK (RESERVATIONS MAY BE NECESSARY). WHEREVER
YOU BED DOWN YOU'RE BOUND TO HAVE SERIOUS FULL-TUCK
DOWNHILL DREAMS AFTER A DAY OF RIDING IN ALPINE COUNTY.

— MONITOR PASS, 8300' – NEARLY 3,000' ABOVE MAR-
KLEEVILLE, IS ON A DRY BACKFOLD OF THE SIERRA. YOU CLIMB
THE SOUTHERN END OF HWY 89 ALONG MONITOR CREEK CANYON
TO HEENAN LAKE AND HIGHER THROUGH GREAT GROVES OF ASPEN.

— EBBETTS PASS AND PACIFIC GRADE SUMMIT, 8,730' AND
8,050', IS A QUIET AND LUSHLY VEGETATED CLIMB. A FIFTY MILE
ROUNDTRIP THAT ADDS UP TO MORE THAN 4,000' OF CLIMBING.

— KINGSBURY GRADE / DAGGETT PASS, 7,334', AFTER
A SMALL CLIMB BETWEEN MARKLEEVILLE AND WOODFORDS
THIS RIDE FOLLOWS THE CARSON RIVER INTO NEVADA, (USE
EMIGRANT TRAIL AND FREDRICKSBURG RD. NORTHWEST OF
STATE HWY 88), A RELATIVELY FLAT RIDE UNTIL NEVADA HWY 206
INTERSECTS WITH HWY 207 IN MOTTSVILLE. TURN WEST ON 207
AND CLIMB (THE KINGSBURY GRADE SECTION IS SAID TO BE AS
STEEP AS 16% – DOESN'T FEEL THAT STEEP.) TO DAGGETT
WHICH OVERLOOKS THE SOUTH LAKE TAHOE METROPOLITAN AREA.

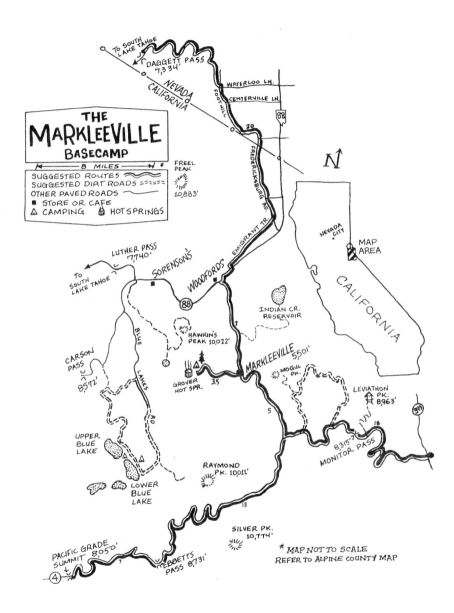

THE
MARKLEEVILLE
BASECAMP

├──── 8 MILES ────┤ *

SUGGESTED ROUTES ～～～
SUGGESTED DIRT ROADS ＝＝＝＝
OTHER PAVED ROADS ～～
■ STORE OR CAFE
△ CAMPING ♨ HOT SPRINGS

TO SOUTH LAKE TAHOE
DAGGETT PASS 7,334'
NEVADA
CALIFORNIA
WATERLOO LN.
CENTERVILLE LN.
FOOT HILL
20
88
FREDERICKSBURG RD.
FREEL PEAK 10,883'
EMIGRANT TR.
N

LUTHER PASS 7,740'
SORENSON'S
WOODFORDS
TO SOUTH LAKE TAHOE
88
INDIAN CR. RESERVOIR
NEVADA CITY
MAP AREA
CALIFORNIA

CARSON PASS 8,572'
BLUE LAKES
HAWKIN'S PEAK 10,022'
GROVER HOT SPR.
3.5
MARKLEEVILLE 5501'
MOGUL PK.
LEVIATHON PK. 8,963'
5
8315' MONITOR PASS
10
18
89

UPPER BLUE LAKE
LOWER BLUE LAKE
RAYMOND PK. 10011'
13

PACIFIC GRADE SUMMIT 8050'
7
EBBETTS PASS 8,731'
SILVER PK. 10,774'
4

* MAP NOT TO SCALE
REFER TO ALPINE COUNTY MAP

35

EL DORADO LOOP

WE START THIS LOOP FROM POLLOCK PINES AT NEARLY 4,000! A QUICK DROP DOWN SLY PARK ROAD AND E-16 TO SOMERSET WHICH SITS AT APPROXIMATELY 2,000'. THREE MILES BEYOND YOU'LL TURN EAST ON FAIRPLAY RD. (A NEW STORE AND CAFE ARE LOCATED HERE). BY THE TIME YOU REACH FAIRPLAY YOU'LL BE REMINDED, AS WE WERE, THAT FOR EVERY DOWNHILL ENJOYED THERE IS DOUBLE THE UPHILL TO BE REPAID.

AT EXACTLY THE HALFWAY POINT OF THE LOOP (ON UPPER OMO RANCH ROAD) YOU'LL FIND THE NASTIEST CATTLE-GUARD IN THE STATE — NOT CROSSABLE AT HIGH SPEED ON SKINNY TIRES! FLAT METAL REINFORCING STRIPS HAVE BEEN WELDED IN A CATTYWOMPUS AND HAPHAZARD FASHION ACROSS THE USUAL PERPENDICULAR BARS FOUND ON MOST GUARDS. THIS IS THE BEST REASON FOR RIDING THE LOOP IN A COUNTERCLOCKWISE DIRECTION (MAKING IT AN UPHILL CROSSING.)

THE NORTH-SOUTH RD. (OLD F.S. 6) IS THE QUIETEST STRETCH OF THE LOOP, A REMOTE ROLLERCOASTER THROUGH SHADY CANYONS AND OVER FORESTED RIDGES — MANY LOCALS DON'T EVEN KNOW THIS IS A THRU ROAD (PAVED).

ONE UNFORTUNATE FACT IS THAT THE HILLS EAST OF SACRAMEN-TO ARE GETTING BUSIER EACH YEAR AT A RATE SYNONYMOUS WITH THE PHENOMENAL GROWTH OF THE SAC. AREA. SCHEDULE YOUR RIDE HERE DURING A WEEKDAY OR OFF-SEASON WEEKEND (BEST DURING AUTUMN).

STARTING POINT—
POLLOCK PINES

DISTANCE — 80 MILES

DIRECTION—
COUNTERCLOCKWISE

HIGH POINT — 5,306'
MORMON EMIGRANT TR.

LOW POINT — 2,000'
SOUTH OF SOMERSET

CAMPING — SLY PARK
AND ALONG NORTH-
SOUTH RD. (F.S. 6)

WINERIES — SOMERSET,
PLEASANT VALLEY

CALIFORNIA

LAKE
TAHOE

AREA
OF
MAP

POLLOCK
PINES
3981'

50
TO
LAKE SO. TAHOE

TO SACRAMENTO
55 MILES

SLY
PARK

3470'

MORMON EMIGRANT

11

CAPP'S CROSSING

TRAIL

RD.

BALTIC
PK.
5,078'

N

E-16
8

TO PLACERVILLE

PLEASANT
VALLEY

5

HAPPY VALLEY RD.

FLAT RD.

GRIZZLY FLAT
3880'

GRIZZLY

EL
DORADO
NATL.
FOREST

NORTH SOUTH RD.

24

SOMERSET
2,090'

3

80
MILE
LOOP

E-16

7.5

FAIRPLAY RD.

FAIRPLAY
2,320'

TO HWY
49

OMO RANCH RD.

14

HAZARDOUS
CATTLE GUARD!

COOK'S
STATION

5,000'

88

ALSO REFER
TO AN
EL DORADO
COUNTY MAP

THE
EL DORADO
LOOP

6 MILES

SUGGESTED ROADS
OTHER INTERESTING ROADS
■ STORES + CAFES
△ CAMPGROUNDS
☀ PEAK

MAP NOT DRAWN
STRICTLY TO SCALE

91

36

GOLD LAKE LOOP

GRAEAGLE, A SOUTHERN PLUMAS COUNTY VILLAGE, GETS MY VOTE AS THE PRIMO PLACE TO 'PARK AND EMBARK' ON THIS LOOP RIDE WHICH IS, IN EFFECT, A 50 MILE RIDE AROUND HASKELL PEAK.

THE ONLY TIME YOU MIGHT ENCOUNTER TRAFFIC ON THIS RIDE WOULD BE DURING A

DISTANCE – 50 MILES	
DIRECTION –	COUNTERCLOCKWISE
HIGH POINT –	GOLD LAKE PASS 6,490'
LOW POINT –	GRAEAGLE 4,385'
LODGING –	WHITE SULPHUR SPRINGS BED AND BREAKFAST ON HIGHWAY 89

HOLIDAY WEEKEND — MORE AND MORE SACRAMENTO VALLEY RESIDENTS ARE "DISCOVERING" THE HEADWATERS OF THE YUBA RIVER AND THE IMPRESSIVE BACKDROP THE SIERRA BUTTES FURNISH FOR A WEEKEND OF CAMPING OR FISHING.

SMALL STORES ARE FOUND IN BASSETTS AND SATTLEY ON HWY 49.

YOU CAN MAKE IT A METRIC CENTURY BY COMPLETING THE 12 MILE OUT AND BACK TO JOHNSVILLE AND GET IN 1000 FT. OF EXTRA CLIMBING! OH, JOY!

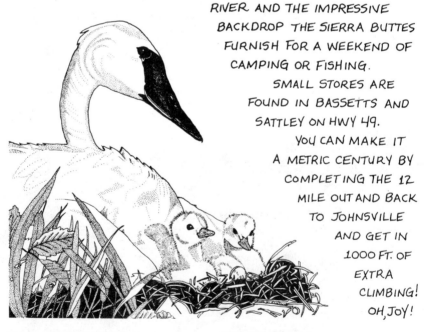

RESIDENTS OF THE MOHAWK VALLEY, NEAR CLIO

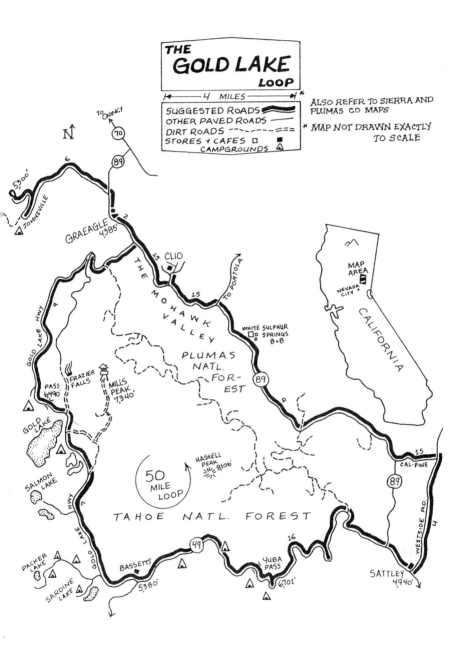

THE
GOLD LAKE
LOOP

|← 4 MILES →|

SUGGESTED ROADS
OTHER PAVED ROADS
DIRT ROADS
STORES + CAFES □
CAMPGROUNDS ⛺

ALSO REFER TO SIERRA AND
PLUMAS CO MAPS

* MAP NOT DRAWN EXACTLY
TO SCALE

N

TO QUINCY
70
89

5300'
6
JOHNSVILLE

GRAEAGLE
4385'
2

1.5 CLIO

TO PORTOLA

1.5

THE MOHAWK VALLEY

WHITE SULPHUR
SPRINGS
B+B

PLUMAS
NATL.
FOR-
EST

89

9

GOLD LAKE HWY
9

PASS
6490'

FRAZIER
FALLS

MILLS
PEAK
7,340'

GOLD
LAKE

SALMON
LAKE

GOLD LAKE HWY

MAP
AREA

NEVADA
CITY

CALIFORNIA

1.5
CAL-PINE
89

50
MILE
LOOP

HASKELL
PEAK
8106'

TAHOE NATL. FOREST

PACKER
LAKE

SARDINE
LAKE

BASSETTS
5,380'

49

16

YUBA
PASS
6701'

WESTSIDE RD.
4

SATTLEY
4,940'

93

37

PLUMAS COUNTY
INDIAN VALLEY

EARLY SUMMER IS A GOOD TIME TO CATCH A LIBERAL SPRINKLING OF WILDFLOWERS HERE AS WELL AS THOUSANDS OF ACRES OF MEADOW IN LUSH GREEN SURROUNDED BY THE LAST PRECIPITOUS FINGERS OF THE SIERRA NEVADA — KEDDIE RIDGE, KETTLE PEAK AND A PICTURESQUE MT. HOUGH.

A REAL CYCLIST'S PLAYGROUND — IF YOU'RE LOOKING FOR INDOOR LODGING YOU COULD USE THE CRESCENT HOTEL IN CRESCENT MILLS OR THE PIONEER IN GREENVILLE AS A BASECAMP FOR A WEEKEND OF EXPLORING SOME OF PLUMAS COUNTY'S QUIETEST BACKROADS. THE PAVED ROADS ON THE FLOOR OF THE INDIAN VALLEY ARE OPEN YEAR 'ROUND BUT YOU MIGHT FIND WINTER RIDING A BIT CHILLY AT 3,500'

I'VE SHOWN YOU A BIT MORE DIRT ON THIS TOUR AND I'VE INCLUDED FOURTEEN MILES OF WELL GROOMED DIRT ROAD ON THE 50 MILE TAYLORSVILLE / ANTELOPE LAKE ROUTE. THIS IS ONE OF THE MANY LOOPS THAT WE CRANKED-OUT IN THE MID '70's ON OUR 27" X 1¼" TIRES, NEVER IMAGINING SUCH A FEAT WOULD BE CONSIDERED A BIG DEAL FOR SKINNY-TIRE BICYCLES — WE ALWAYS KNEW OUR BICYCLES COULD TAKE US MOST ANYWHERE. LITTLE DID WE KNOW THAT FLAT HANDLE BARS AND FATTER TIRES WERE ABOUT TO "REVOLUTIONIZE" THE BICYCLE INDUSTRY AND MAKE A FEW BAY AREA WHIZ-KIDS... BAY AREA MARKETING WHIZ-KIDS, EXCEEDINGLY WEALTHY.

DISTANCE - 34 AND 50 MI.

DIRECTION -
COUNTERCLOCKWISE ON BOTH LOOPS

HIGH POINT -
LONE ROCK VALLEY 5,412'

LOW POINT -
CRESCENT MILLS 3,515'

GROCERIES -
GENERAL STORE IN TAYLORSVILLE AND MARKETS IN GREENVILLE

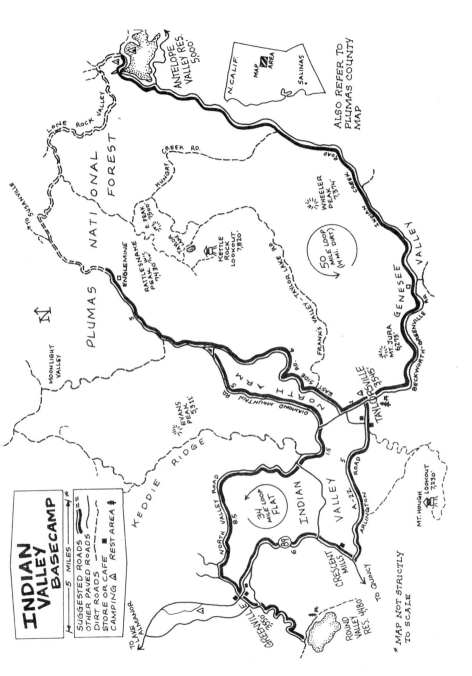

INDIAN VALLEY BASECAMP

─5 MILES─

SUGGESTED ROADS
OTHER PAVED ROADS
DIRT ROADS
STORE OR CAFE ▪
CAMPING ⛺ REST AREA ⛐

N

PLUMAS NATIONAL FOREST

MOON LIGHT VALLEY

TO SUSANVILLE

LONE ROCK VALLEY

ANTELOPE VALLEY RES. 5,000'

N. CALIF.
MAP AREA
SALINAS

ALSO REFER TO PLUMAS COUNTY MAP

HUNGRY CREEK RD.

ENGLEMINE

RATTLESNAKE PEAK 7,130'

E. PEAK 7,500'

TAYLOR CREEK RD.

KETTLE ROCK LOOKOUT 7,820'

WHEELER PEAK 7,374'

50 LOOP MILE (HI. MI. DIRT)

FRANK'S VALLEY

TAYLOR LAKE RD.

GENESEE VALLEY

INDIAN CREEK

BECKWORTH-GREENVILLE RD.

MT. JURA 6,275'

TAYLORSVILLE 3,545'

EAST SIDE RD.

DIAMOND MOUNTAIN RD.

NORTH ARM

EVANS PEAK 5,311'

KEDDIE RIDGE

NORTH VALLEY ROAD

8.5

34 LOOP MILE FLAT

89

6

INDIAN VALLEY

1.5

5

A-22 ROAD

ARLINGTON

MT. HOUGH LOOKOUT 7,330'

CRESCENT MILLS

TO QUINCY

GREENVILLE 3,550'

TO LAKE ALMANOR

ROUND VALLEY RES. 4,480'

* MAP NOT STRICTLY TO SCALE

95

38
PLUMAS COUNTY
CHESTER BASECAMP

THE FLATTEST RIDE IN THIS GUIDE IS THE LOOP AROUND LAKE ALMANOR — SO WHY DO I CHOSE SUCH TAME TERRAIN FOR MY BACKYARD?... GOOD QUESTION.

THERE ARE HILLS OUT OF THE LAKE ALMANOR BASIN, HOWEVER, ONLY FIVE OF THEM ARE QUIET PAVED ROADS — YET, THIS

> DISTANCE — TOTAL MAX. 123 MILES
>
> DIRECTION — LAKE LOOP COUNTERCLOCKWISE
>
> HIGH POINT — 6200' ON THE "10 ROAD"
>
> LOW POINT — 4100' BUTT LAKE
>
> CAMPING — NUMEROUS SITES AROUND THE LAKE

SHOULD BE ENOUGH TO ENTERTAIN YOU FOR THE WEEKEND.

LET'S SAY YOU WANT TO GIVE THESE RIDES A TRY — YOU CALL AHEAD AND MAKE RESERVATIONS AT THE 'CINNAMON TEAL' BED AND BREAKFAST (916-258-3993) — FIRST MORNING YOU HEAD UP FEATHER RIVER DRIVE AND RIDE ALL THREE PAVED FORKS LEADING NORTH (SEE MAP) TO DOMINGO SPRS., DRAKESBAD AND TO THE END OF THE PAVEMENT ON JUNIPER LAKE RD. — A GOOD DAY'S WORK, ALMOST 43 MILES AND OVER 2000 FT. OF CLIMBING. AFTER LUNCH YOU DISCOVER NEW ENERGY AND DESIRE, SO YOU HOP IN THE SADDLE AND ROAR EASTWARD ON HWY 36 (DO IT BEFORE 2PM — THIS ROAD GETS BUSY AT 3PM), THEN TURN NORTH ON THE ROAD TO THE DUMP AND ANOTHER QUICK LEFT WHERE THE ROAD COMES TO A "T." HERE BEGINS "THE 10 ROAD" WHICH HEADS TOWARD THE CARIBOU WILDERNESS, CONTINUE TO THE END OF THE PAVEMENT AND RETURN — A 32 MILE RIDE — ADDING UP TO OVER 75 FOR THE DAY. REST UP, EAT A BIG PASTA DINNER — TOMORROW WILL BE A PIECE O' CAKE.

SECOND DAY — THE LOOP AROUND THE LAKE COULD BE A SIMPLE AND RELATIVELY FLAT 34 MILES OR A MORE INVOLVED 48 mi. RIDE INCLUDING THE BUTT LAKE AND STOVER RDS.

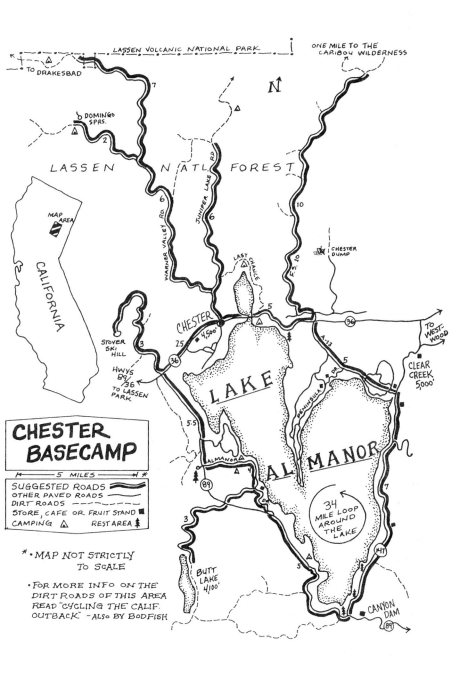

LASSEN VOLCANIC NATIONAL PARK

ONE MILE TO THE
CARIBOU WILDERNESS

TO DRAKESBAD

7

DOMINGO
SPRS.

2

N

LASSEN   N A T L.   FOREST

MAP
AREA

CALIFORNIA

WARNER VALLEY RD.
6

JUNIPER LAKE RD.
6

10

F.S. 10

CHESTER
DUMP

LAST
CHANCE

5

STOVER
SKI
HILL

3

CHESTER
4,500'

2.5

36

HWYS
89/36
TO LASSEN
PARK

TO
WEST-
WOOD

36

A-13

5

CLEAR
CREEK
5,000'

LAKE

PENINSULA
DR.

5.5

A L M A N O R

7

34
MILE LOOP
AROUND
THE
LAKE

ALMANOR

89

DR.

3

BUTT
LAKE
4,100'

5

H-7

CANYON
DAM

89

CHESTER BASECAMP

— 5 MILES — *

SUGGESTED ROADS
OTHER PAVED ROADS
DIRT ROADS
STORE, CAFE OR FRUIT STAND ▪
CAMPING △   REST AREA 🏕

* • MAP NOT STRICTLY
    TO SCALE

• FOR MORE INFO ON THE
  DIRT ROADS OF THIS AREA
  READ "CYCLING THE CALIF.
  OUTBACK" - ALSO BY BODFISH

39, 39A

TEHAMA AND SHASTA COUNTIES

ALPINE-CASCADE, LMMC*

THIS IS IT! THE BEST ROAD RIDE IN CALIFORNIA. LASSEN VOLCANIC NATIONAL PARK IS THE LONELIEST NATIONAL PARK IN THE STATE OF CALIFORNIA AND THERE-FORE ONE OF THE QUIETEST SCENIC SPOTS TO BE PEDAL-ING IN THE GOLDEN STATE.

THE PARK ROAD (WHICH CLIMBS TO 8,512') IS GENERALLY OPEN FROM MEMORIAL DAY TO MID-NOVEMBER. DURING THAT SIX MONTH PERIOD ONE MIGHT FIND A LITTLE EXTRA TRAFFIC DURING THE WEEKENDS BETWEEN THE 4th OF JULY AND LABOR DAY. I SUGGEST PICKING A DAY IN JUNE, SEPTEMBER OR OCTOBER FOR EITHER OF THE RIDES MAPPED HERE.

* THE LASSEN MTN. METRIC CENTURY (39A) IS THE FINEST "HYBRID" RIDE I'VE FOUND — 23 MILES OF DIRT AND 39 MILES OF PAVEMENT WHICH INCLUDE VIEWS OF MT. SHASTA, THE SACRAMENTO VALLEY, MANZANITA LAKE, CHAOS CRAGS, LAKE ALMANOR, HOT SPRINGS VALLEY AND THE SNOWY SHOULDER OF 10,457' LASSEN PEAK.

THE PARK ENTRANCE FEE IS NOW (1990) $2.00 PER CYCLIST — IF YOU LIVE WITHIN ONE HUNDRED MILES OF THE PARK IT PAYS TO BUY A LASSEN PARK SEASON PASS.

IF A SEGMENT OF YOUR FAMILY ENJOYS HIK-ING AS MUCH AS YOU LOVE CYCLING, PARK AT THE CHALET AND CRANK OUT A 60 MILE OUT AND BACK TO MANZANITA LAKE WHILE THE OTHERS EXPLORE LASSEN'S TRAILS.

STARTING POINT— FOR BOTH RIDES - MINERAL

DISTANCE — ALL PAVEMENT 82 MILES. HYBRID LOOP 62 Mi.

DIRECTION — CLOCKWISE ON MOUNTAIN METRIC CENTURY.

HIGH POINT— 8512' LASSEN PARK RD. SUMMIT

LOW POINT— 4,798' MINERAL

LODGING — MINERAL, CHILD'S MEADOWS, CHESTER

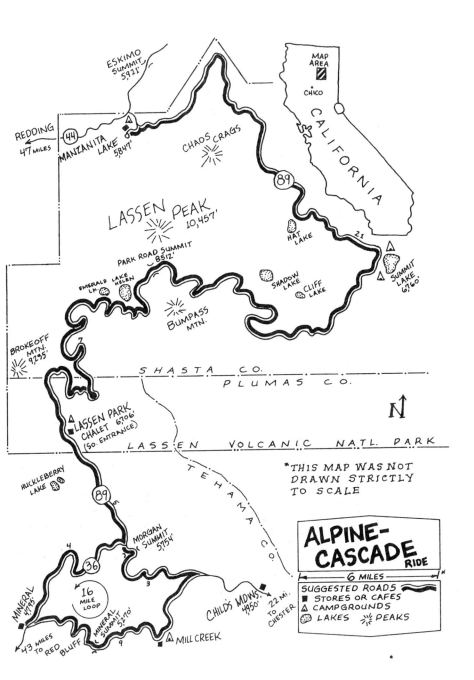

ESKIMO SUMMIT 5,921'

MAP AREA

CHICO

CALIFORNIA

REDDING 47 MILES

44

MANZANITA LAKE 5,847'

CHAOS CRAGS

89

LASSEN PEAK 10,457'

HAT LAKE

21

PARK ROAD SUMMIT 8512'

EMERALD LK.

LAKE HELEN

SHADOW LAKE

CLIFF LAKE

SUMMIT LAKE 6,760'

BUMPASS MTN.

BROKEOFF MTN. 9,235'

7

SHASTA CO.

PLUMAS CO.

N↑

LASSEN PARK CHALET 6706' (So. ENTRANCE)

LASSEN VOLCANIC NATL. PARK

HUCKLEBERRY LAKE

89

TEHAMA CO.

*THIS MAP WAS NOT DRAWN STRICTLY TO SCALE

MORGAN SUMMIT 5,754'

4

36

16 MILE LOOP

3

MINERAL 4,795'

MINERAL SUMMIT 5,170'

9

CHILDS MDWS. 4,950'

22 Mi. TO CHESTER

ALPINE-CASCADE RIDE

6 MILES

SUGGESTED ROADS
■ STORES OR CAFES
▲ CAMPGROUNDS
◉ LAKES
☀ PEAKS

43 MILES TO RED BLUFF

▲ MILL CREEK

99

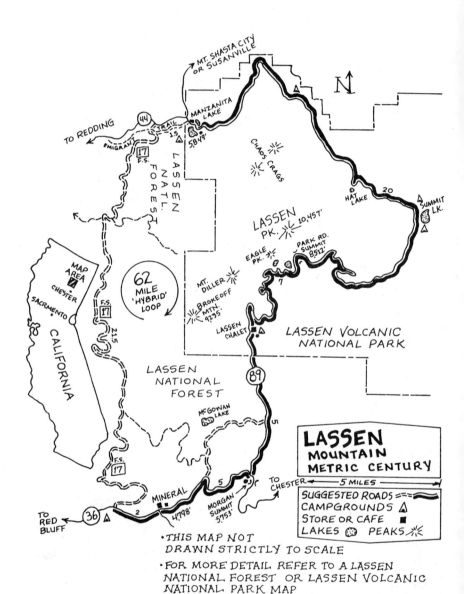

MT. SHASTA CITY
OR SUSANVILLE

N

TO REDDING

44

MANZANITA
LAKE

TRAIL
1.5
EMIGRANT

5,849'

17
F.S.

LASSEN NATL. FOREST

CHAOS CRAGS

HAT LAKE

20

SUMMIT LK.

LASSEN PK. 10,457'

EAGLE PK.

PARK RD.
SUMMIT
8512'

MT. DILLER

7

62
MILE
'HYBRID'
LOOP

MAP AREA

CHESTER

SACRAMENTO

F.S.
17

21.5

CALIFORNIA

BROKEOFF
MTN.
9235'

LASSEN
CHALET

LASSEN VOLCANIC
NATIONAL PARK

LASSEN
NATIONAL
FOREST

McGOWAN LAKE

89

5

F.S.
17

MINERAL

4,798'

2

MORGAN
SUMMIT
5,753'

5

TO CHESTER

36

TO RED BLUFF

LASSEN
MOUNTAIN
METRIC CENTURY

5 MILES

SUGGESTED ROADS
CAMPGROUNDS △
STORE OR CAFE ■
LAKES ☺ PEAKS ☀

• THIS MAP NOT
DRAWN STRICTLY TO SCALE

• FOR MORE DETAIL REFER TO A LASSEN
NATIONAL FOREST OR LASSEN VOLCANIC
NATIONAL PARK MAP

40

SISKIYOU AND SHASTA COUNTIES

SHASTA VIEW

TRUELY "IN THE SHADOW OF SHASTA", THIS FAR CORNER OF CALIFORNIA LOOP EXPOSES YOU TO SOME OF THE RAREST GEOLOGY, MOST INCREDIBLE VIEWS AND QUIETEST ROADS IN SISKIYOU COUNTY.

> STARTING POINT—
> HARRIS SPRINGS
> ON F.S. 15
> DISTANCE — 60 MILES
> DIRECTION —
> CLOCKWISE
> HIGH POINT — 7,206'
> LOW POINT — 4,586'
> CAMPING — HARRIS SPR.
> AND MEDICINE LAKE

EVEN THOUGH I PREFER RIDING THE REMOTE HILLS OF SISKIYOU, SHASTA, MODOC, LASSEN AND PLUMAS COUNTIES OVER THOSE IN ANY OTHER REGION OF THE STATE, I MUST SAY, I'M HONESTLY RELIEVED WHEN I SEE A PICK-UP TRUCK COMING MY WAY IN THESE AREAS. THERE ARE MANY ROADS OUT THERE THAT DON'T SEE TRAFFIC FOR SEVERAL DAYS ON END AND (WE DON'T LIKE TO TALK ABOUT IT BUT...) IF I HAD A SERIOUS BREAKDOWN IN BODY, BIKE OR SPIRIT WHILE WANDERING THIS PORTION OF THE CALIFORNIA OUTBACK HELP MIGHT BE A LONG TIME IN COMING.

WEATHER AND ROAD CONDITIONS ARE UNPREDICTABLE IN THIS HIGH PLATEAU REGION, SO BE WISE, USE FAT TIRES AND CARRY: A TARP, FOOD, A SLEEPING BAG, MATCHES, RAIN GEAR AND A SET OF DRY CLOTHES WHEN SETTING OUT ON A LENGTHY RIDE IN A REMOTE AREA.

THERE ISN'T A RESTAURANT, GAS STATION OR GROCERY WITHIN SEVERAL MILES OF THIS LOOP. IT WOULD, HOWEVER, BE QUITE CONVENIENT TO FIND LODGING IN MT. SHASTA CITY OR McCLOUD.

BE SURE TO NOTE THAT SIX MILES OF THIS LOOP ARE ON AN UNPAVED ROADWAY — NECESSITATING FAT TIRES.

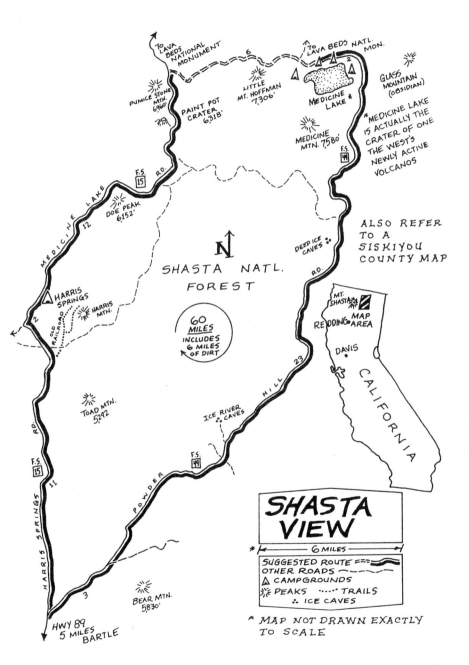

TO LAVA BEDS NATIONAL MONUMENT

TO LAVA BEDS NATL. MON.

PUMICE STONE MTN. 6,960'

PAINT POT CRATER 6,318'

LITTLE MT. HOFFMAN 7,306'

MEDICINE LAKE *

GLASS MOUNTAIN (OBSIDIAN)

MEDICINE MTN. 7,580'

* MEDICINE LAKE IS ACTUALLY THE CRATER OF ONE THE WEST'S NEWLY ACTIVE VOLCANOS

F.S. 15

DOE PEAK 6,152'

MEDICINE LAKE

12

F.S. 14

DEEP ICE CAVES

ALSO REFER TO A SISKIYOU COUNTY MAP

N

SHASTA NATL. FOREST

HARRIS SPRINGS

OLD RAILROAD

HARRIS MTN.

2

RD.

MT. SHASTA

REDDING

MAP AREA

DAVIS

60 MILES
INCLUDES 6 MILES OF DIRT

CALIFORNIA

HILL 23

TOAD MTN. 5,292'

ICE RIVER CAVES

F.S. 15

11

POWDER

F.S. 49

HARRIS SPRINGS RD.

3

BEAR MTN. 5,830'

HWY 89 5 MILES BARTLE

SHASTA VIEW

* |——— 6 MILES ———|

SUGGESTED ROUTE ═══
OTHER ROADS ∼∼∼
△ CAMPGROUNDS
☀ PEAKS ⋯⋯ TRAILS
∴ ICE CAVES

* MAP NOT DRAWN EXACTLY TO SCALE

TEN BIKE RIDES THAT ALMOST CUT THE MUSTARD

ORIGINALLY, I HAD FIFTY PAVED LOOPS SCOUTED FOR THIS EDITION OF CALIFORNIA DREAM CYCLING, HOWEVER AFTER RERIDING MANY OF THE LOOPS AND DISCUSSING THEIR FEATURES WITH VARIOUS RIDING BUDDIES, I HONED THIS LIST OF "DREAM RIDES" DOWN TO THE FORTY MAPPED IN THIS BOOK.

YET, HERE I AM, READY TO GO TO PRESS, BUT I STILL FEEL IT WOULD BE VALUABLE TO MENTION THE TEN CIRCUITS THAT VERY NEARLY MADE THE GRADE. THEY ARE GREAT RIDES WITH ONLY MINOR PROBLEMS.

41 CARMEL VALLEY – ARROYO SECO – RIVER RD. LOOP
ROADS G-16,17 • 102 MILES —MONTEREY COUNTY

THE CARMEL / MONTEREY END OF THIS LOOP IS A MESS TRAFFICWISE, THERE ARE EVEN A FEW MILES OF FREEWAY BIKING THAT SEEM UNAVOIDABLE. CARMEL VALLEY RD. (G-16) HAS BECOME A POPULAR COMMUTER ROUTE AND DOESN'T MELLOW-OUT TRAFFIC-WISE UNTIL YOU ARE TWELVE MILES SOUTH OF CARMEL. THE SOUTH HALF OF THIS LOOP IS ESPECIALLY BLISSFUL DURING A WEEKDAY IN EARLY SPRING.

42 THE LOCKWOOD / LAKE SAN ANTONIO FIGURE EIGHT
ROADS G-14, 18, 19 • 90 MILES — MONTEREY COUNTY

WE WERE SURPRIZED TO FIND HIGH SPEED AND FREQUENT TRAFFIC ON JOLON RD. (G-14). IT MAY HAVE JUST BEEN AN EXCEPTIONALLY BUSY WEEKEND DUE TO MANUEVERS AT FORT HUNTER LIGGETT. AVOID THIS AREA DURING SUMMER WEEKENDS.

43 MAPLE CREEK – FRESHWATER RD. LOOP
• 48 MILES — HUMBOLDT COUNTY

HONESTLY, I HAVE FORGOTTEN WHY I SET
THIS LOOP ON THE BACK BURNER. WINDING YOUR WAY
THROUGH ARCATA CAN BE A LITTLE HECTIC, YET THE HASSLE
IS MINIMAL WHEN COMPARED TO WHAT MOST URBAN
CALIFORNIANS TOLERATE DURING AN AVERAGE WEEK-
END RIDE. DURING THE SUMMER MONTHS THE COASTAL
AREA FOG IS SUFFOCATING — THIS SERVES TO MAKE THE
RIDE ALL THE MORE SATISFYING WHEN YOU PULL
YOURSELF OUT OF THE THICK SOUP TO RIDGETOPS
BASKING IN 70° SUNSHINE.

44 SCOTT RIVER CANYON – KLAMATH RIVER – YREKA LOOP
HWYS 3, 96 AND 263 • 90 MILE LOOP – SISKIYOU CO.

HEADING SOUTH OUT OF YREKA CAN BE A BIT
HARROWING. ONCE YOU'VE CROSSED FOREST MOUNTAIN
SUMMIT (A 1500 FT. CLIMB), IT'S A SMOOTH SLIDE DOWN
TO FORT JONES — WHERE YOU TURN RIGHT AND FOLLOW
THE SCOTT RIVER VALLEY TO THE FOREBODING AND PRE-
CIPITOUS SCOTT RIVER CANYON. AT THE HWY 96 JUNCTION
TURN RIGHT AGAIN. TO AVOID RIDING THE MAIN KLAMATH
RIVER HWY, (WHICH AT TIMES, CARRIES A REGULAR PRO-
CESSION OF LARGE TRUCKS), TURN RIGHT ON WALKER
ROAD (JUST BEYOND HORSE CREEK) FOR THE NEXT 25 Mi.
STAY ON THE SOUTH SIDE OF THE RIVER — THIS ROAD
SURFACE MAY BE LESS IDEAL FOR SKINNY TIRES ABOVE
THE SLEEPY SETTLEMENT OF WALKER.

45 FEATHER FALLS – LITTLE GRASS VALLEY LOOP
• 60 MILES – BUTTE AND PLUMAS CO.

FROM THE SMALL VILLAGE OF FEATHER FALLS
FOLLOW LUMPKIN – LA PORTE ROAD AND RETURN VIA

LUMPKIN RIDGE ROAD. A VERY REMOTE METRIC CENTURY LOOP FIRST PINPOINTED BY THE CHICO VELO CYCLING CLUB.

46 THE CORNING – PASKENTA – BLACK BUTTE LOOP
A-9, NEWVILLE RD., BLACK BUTTE RD • 55 MILES
TEHAMA AND GLENN COUNTIES.

A GREAT WESTSIDE LOOP TO THE DRAMATIC FOLDS NEAR THE WESTERN EDGE OF THE NORTH AMERICAN PLATE. HERE THE WILDFLOWERS SURPRIZE AND ASTOUND THE OBSERVANT TRAVELER FROM LATE FEBRUARY THROUGH APRIL. SOME ROLLER COASTER HILLS AND SIX MILES OF DIRT AND GRAVEL MAKE THIS A CHALLENGING CIRCUIT. I'VE SHIED AWAY FROM PROMOTING THIS RIDE DUE TO EFFORTS TO LOCATE A CLASS II HAZARDOUS WASTE SITE SOMEWHERE ALONG BLACK BUTTE ROAD.

47 THE PINE FLAT – DINKEY CREEK CENTURY LOOP
• 100 MILES – FRESNO COUNTY

EXPLORING THE FOOTHILLS BETWEEN THE SAN JOAQUIN AND KINGS RIVERS. IT'S BEEN TEN OR MORE YEARS SINCE I RODE THIS LOOP. WE CAMPED ON PINE FLAT RESERVOIR AND RODE UP THE NORTH FORK OF THE KINGS RIVER (THIS ROAD WAS GREATLY IMPROVED IN THE LATE 70'S WHEN P.G and E. DEVELOPED THE HELMS POWER PROJECT BETWEEN COURTRIGHT AND WISHON RESERVOIRS).

THE STRETCH OF ROAD THAT KEPT THIS LOOP OUT OF THE "TOP FORTY" IS THE 6 MILE SECTION OF HWY 168 BETWEEN SHAVER LAKE AND PINE RIDGE. EXIT TOWARD TOLLHOUSE AND TAKE LEFTS ON BURROUGHS VALLEY, MAXON AND TRIMMER SPRINGS ROAD.

48 THE BUCK'S LAKE LOOP • 18 MILES
TEN MILES WEST OF QUINCY — PLUMAS COUNTY
A SHORT, BUT UNIQUE LOOP THAT INCLUDES
2,000 FT. OF CLIMBING ON A CLASSIC 18% GRADE TO BUCK'S
SUMMIT. RIDE THIS ONE IN COUNTERCLOCKWISE DIRECTION.

49 THE EAGLE LAKE LOOP • 75 MILES
HWY 36 — A 1 — HWY 139 — LASSEN COUNTY
THIS RIDE BEGINS IN SUSANVILLE WITH A MOD-
ERATELY BUSY CLIMB ON HWY 36, (RIDE THIS LOOP IN A
CLOCKWISE DIRECTION), TURN NORTH ON COUNTY ROAD
A·1 TOWARD EAGLE LAKE.
LASSEN VELO CYCLING CLUB RUNS A ROAD
RACE ALONG THIS CIRCUIT EACH SUMMER. FOLLOW THE
WEST AND NORTH SHORES OF EAGLE LAKE TO STATE HWY
139 (NOT THE GREATEST CYCLING ROAD) AND RETURN
SOUTH TO SUSANVILLE.

50 WARNER MOUNTAINS
HWY 299 — SURPRISE VALLEY ROAD
MODOC COUNTY
THE ROAD RIDING IS SOMEWHAT LIMITED HERE
BY THE FACT THAT THERE ARE NO PAVED LOOPS. YET, AN OUT-
AND BACK STROLL ALONG SURPRIZE VALLEY ROAD MAY LIFT
YOUR SPIRITS AND FILL YOUR SENSES — BRINGING ON A
PERMANENT SMILE , IT SURE DOES THIS FOR TEAM
BODFISH. FOR MANY OF YOU, THE LONG DRIVE TO THIS
REMOTE CORNER OF CALIFORNIA MAY NOT BE WORTH
THE LIMITED AMOUNT OF PAVED ROAD RIDING AVAILABLE
HERE.

INDEX

EPILOGUE

AFTER TWENTY YEARS OF WANDERING THE CALIFORNIA OUTBACK BY BICYCLE, I'VE FOUND MOST OF THE QUIET ROADS IN THE STATE. IN THIS SEARCH I HAVE ALSO BEEN EXPOSED TO CALIFORNIA'S WORST AND BUSIEST ROADS, (WHICH ARE, BY THE WAY, BECOMING MORE NUMEROUS EACH YEAR). THIS IS THE FOURTH BICYCLE GUIDE WE'VE PUBLISHED IN THE LAST DOZEN YEARS AND IT IS THE MOST COMPREHENSIVE.

NOT ALL OF THE GOLDEN STATES QUIET LANES ARE INCLUDED HERE BECAUSE I'VE MADE AN ATTEMPT TO FIT THE QUIETEST ROADS INTO "DREAM LOOPS". I'VE AVOIDED MANY OF THE FLATLAND AND DESERT RIDES THAT ARE OUT THERE SO THAT THOSE OF YOU WHO USE THIS BOOK WILL BE EXPOSED TO THE LUSHEST SCENERY AND THE LEAST AMOUNT OF SMOG AND AGRICULTURAL POLLUTION AS IS POSSIBLE. BESIDES, WE LOVE HILLS AND FROM THE LETTERS WE'VE RECEIVED OVER THE LAST DOZEN YEARS, WE BELIEVE YOU LOVE HILLS.

IF YOU CAN SUGGEST ANY ROADS OR LOOPS FOR US TO INCLUDE IN FUTURE EDITIONS, PLEASE WRITE:
TEAM BODFISH — P.O. BOX 69 CHESTER, CA. 96020

C. "BODFISH" ELLIOT

P.S. HANDLETTERING (MUCH LIKE BICYCLING) IS NOT NECESSARILY AN AVOIDANCE OF "MODERN" TECHNOLOGY AND GADGETRY, BUT RATHER A SELF-POWERED WAY TO CREATE.

FOR ADDITIONAL COPIES OF

CALIFORNIA DREAM CYCLING

SEND $12.50 (PRICE INCLUDES TAX AND SHIPPING) TO:
BODFISH P.O. BOX 69
CHESTER, CA. 96020

---

also available: BODFISH'S POPULAR OFF-ROAD GUIDE

CYCLING THE CALIFORNIA OUTBACK

21 MAPS — 68 PAGES
RECENTLY UPDATED.
SHOULD BE AVAILABLE AT YOUR
FAVORITE BICYCLE SHOP — OR
ORDER DIRECTLY FROM THE
AUTHOR — SEND $6.50 PLUS $1.
SHIPPING TO BODFISH
P.O. BOX 69
CHESTER, CA. 96020